THE OPEN MEDIA PAMPHLET SERIES

OTHER OPEN MEDIA PAMPHLET SERIES TITLES

CORPORATE MEDIA AND THE THREAT TO DEMOCRACY
Robert W. McChesney
80 pages / $5.95 / ISBN: 1-888363-47-9

MEDIA CONTROL: THE SPECTACULAR ACHIEVEMENTS
OF PROPAGANDA Noam Chomsky
64 pages / $5.95 / ISBN: 1-888363-49-5

GENE WARS: THE POLITICS OF BIOTECHNOLOGY
Kristin Dawkins
64 pages / $4.95 / ISBN: 1-888363-48-7

GLOBALIZING CIVIL SOCIETY: RECLAIMING OUR RIGHT
TO POWER David C. Korten
80 pages / $5.95 / ISBN: 1-888363-59-2

ZAPATISTA ENCUENTRO: DOCUMENTS FROM THE
1996 ENCOUNTER FOR HUMANITY AND AGAINST NEOLIBERALISM
The Zapatistas
64 pages / $5.95 / ISBN: 1-888363-58-4

PROPAGANDA, INC.: SELLING AMERICA'S CULTURE
TO THE WORLD Nancy Snow
80 pages / $5.95 / ISBN: 1-888363-74-6

A SUSTAINABLE ECONOMY FOR THE 21ST CENTURY
Juliet Schor
64 pages / $5.95 / ISBN: 1-888363-75-4

THE UMBRELLA OF U.S. POWER
Noam Chomsky
80 pages / $5.95 / 1-888363-85-1

ACTS OF AGGRESSION: POLICING "ROGUE STATES"
Noam Chomsky, Edward W. Said, Ramsey Clark
64 pages / $6.95 / ISBN: 1-58322-005-4

THE PROGRESSIVE GUIDE TO
ALTERNATIVE MEDIA AND ACTIVISM
Project Censored
144 pages / $10.00 / ISBN: 1-888363-84-3

MICRORADIO AND DEMOCRACY
Greg Ruggiero
64 pages / $5.95 / ISBN: 1-58322-000-3

THE LAST ENERGY WAR: THE BATTLE OVER UTILITY DEREGULATION
Harvey Wasserman
80 pages / $5.95 / ISBN: 1-58322-017-8

POEMS FOR THE NATION: A COLLECTION OF CONTEMPORARY
POLITICAL POEMS Edited by Allen Ginsberg with Andy Clausen and Eliot Katz
80 pages / $5.95 / ISBN: 1-58322-012-7

TO ORDER ADDITIONAL SERIES TITLES CALL 1 (800) 596-7437

THE OPEN MEDIA PAMPHLET SERIES

It's the Media, Stupid

JOHN NICHOLS AND
ROBERT W. McCHESNEY

Introductions by Barbara Ehrenreich,
Ralph Nader, Senator Paul Wellstone

SEVEN STORIES PRESS / New York

A Seven Stories Press First Edition
Open Media Pamphlet Series editor Greg Ruggiero.

Seven Stories Press, 140 Watts Street, New York, NY 10013;
www.sevenstories.com and www. sevenstories.com/textbook

In Canada:
Hushion House, 36 Northline Road, Toronto, Ontario M4B 3E2

In the U.K.:
Turnaround Publisher Services Ltd., Unit 3, Olympia Trading Estate,
Coburg Road, Wood Green, London N22 6TZ

In Australia:
Tower Books, 9/19 Rodborough Road, Frenchs Forest NSW 2086

LIBRARY OF CONGRESS CATALOGING-IN-PUBLICATION DATA
Nichols, John.
It's the media, stupid / John Nichols and Robert W. McChesney.
p. cm. — (Open media pamphlet series; 17)
ISBN 1-58322-029-1 (pbk.)
1. Mass media—United States. 2. Mass media—Social aspects. 3. Communication, International. I. McChesney, Robert Waterman, 1952– II. Title. III. Series.
P92.U5 N53 2000
302.23'0973—dc21 00-020252

College professors may order examination copies of Seven Stories Press titles for a free six-month trial period. To order, visit www.sevenstories.com/textbook, or fax on school letterhead to (212) 226-1411.

Book design by Cindy LaBreacht
9 8 7 6 5 4 3 2 1
Printed in Canada

CONTENTS

INTRODUCTIONS

By Barbara Ehrenreich **7**

By Ralph Nader **11**

By Senator Paul Wellstone **15**

IT'S THE MEDIA, STUPID **21**

CHAPTER 1
The Problem with the U.S. Media **27**

CHAPTER 2
Global Media and Its Discontents **53**

CHAPTER 3
Making Media an Issue in American Politics **89**

Notes **121**

About the Authors **128**

INTRODUCTION BY BARBARA EHRENREICH

Whatever concerns motivate you as a citizen—education, tax policy, health care, gay rights, campaign finance reform—there is no escaping the media. Run a candidate for office, and you'll have to hope her message doesn't get lost when it's squeezed into the increasingly microscopic sound bites favored by TV news. Stage a protest demonstration, and you must worry about whether it will get any coverage—or whether the coverage it gets will turn out to be so warped that you'll wish the media hadn't covered it at all. Or maybe you just want to educate the public about an issue you're all fired up about. Where are you going to turn if not to the media? There's just no other way to communicate with large numbers of other people—to make a point, raise an issue, and begin to flex your muscles as a free citizen of a democratic nation.

The media are as inescapable and ubiquitous a presence in our lives as the environment. In fact, they are, to a large extent, the mental and cultural environment we inhabit every day, bringing us the first voices we hear in the morning, the opinions we absorb while driving, the stories and images that entertain us after work. Insofar as we are intelligent social beings, the media are the world we share.

But the media are more than just an "environment" or a kind of neutral space where ideas, images, and opinions compete for our attention. In the last few years, the media have become a contentious issue in their own right. There's a groundswell of public concern about violence in the media, which may be useful for capturing the attention of channel-surfers but almost certainly seems to have a morally desensitizing effect on the viewer. There's a growing worry about the impact of relentless media-transmitted advertising, especially on children but ultimately on all of us as the advertising slops over into the "content" of a program or an article. And we are just beginning to understand all the ways the news media, in particular, subtly shape public policy and debate: Sensationalized crime coverage, for example, lays the groundwork for grotesquely punitive criminal justice measures like "three strikes and you're out." Grossly inadequate coverage of foreign news leaves us increasingly clueless in an era of globalization.

The problem has always been what to do about it. We can write cranky letters to the editor; we can turn off our TVs. But these are tiny gestures. How can we really affect something as pervasive and powerful—vast, and at the same time, intimate—as the media environment we live in? Here's where Robert McChesney and John Nichols come in. What they show in *It's the Media, Stupid* is that control of the media is becoming a political issue in countries all over the world—a subject for debate and potentially for legislation. It can happen here too, if we are willing to take the next step beyond griping: We can build a grassroots movement to counter the sleaze, the distortions, and the mind-numbing materialism of our unaccountable and corporate-dominated media.

Imagine the kind of media that a democratic society deserves: Media that bring us a wealth of diverse opinions and entertainment options; media that are held responsible for providing us with the information we need to function as informed citizens; media where ideas flow in both directions, and where ordinary people routinely have a chance to voice their concerns. If you like that picture, put yourself into it today by joining the struggle for media reform. McChesney and Nichols have shown us what is possible; now it falls to all of us to realize that potential with our activism.

INTRODUCTION BY RALPH NADER

In Salt Lake City recently, I opened a press conference by looking into the television cameras and talking about the fact that the people, not the multinational communications corporations, own the airwaves.

That's one way to make media an issue. But, as Bob McChesney and John Nichols point out, it's not the only way. In countries around the world, trade unionists, indigenous people, political activists, and ordinary citizens have put media on the agenda. Now, argue McChesney and Nichols, we the people of the United States need to make media a part of the national debate in the land where the founders guaranteed freedom of the press because they knew democracy required rich and diverse sources of information and ideas.

McChesney and Nichols are right.

We all need to start talking about the fact that the people of the United States own the broadcast airwaves; they're the landlords. The radio and the television stations are the tenants. The corporations that own those stations should be paying the FCC for the airwaves and some of that money should be recycled into developing television for the people. The rent money should be paying for audience-run networks that serve the people, that serve democracy, that treat serious matters in engrossing ways.

We all need to start talking about the fact that multinational corporations should not be allowed to dictate to the government the limits that will be placed on competition in the broadcast and print media sectors. We all need to start talking about the power that the people have to use existing anti-trust and broadcast regulations—as well as new laws and new technologies—to break up monopolies and open up a true, wide-ranging democratic dialogue in this country.

There are corporate supremacists who say that issues of media ownership and content are too complex, too abstract to be issues for political debate. But the big corporatists, and those who make apologies for them, are not talking to the people.

When I bring up media issues with citizens in Salt Lake City and Atlanta, Detroit and Nashville, Los Angeles and Denver, I always find that the people get it. They get it 100 percent.

People know the media are betraying their public trust. Whether it's what's on the TV—the exploitation, the commercialism—or the news and public-service programming that isn't on the TV, people know that what they're getting is not what they want or need. When I bring the discussion down to a question of what is and what isn't being covered on the evening news in their own neighborhoods and communities—when I go through how the local news breaks up the thirty minutes: the packaged crime news, the sports, the weather, the phony chit chat—it all connects with what people instinctually know about the disproportionate allocation of television news time.

When anyone talks about what's wrong with media today, and about how citizens should have the power to make meaningful change, people get excited. People like the idea of controlling some of what they own, and they're pretty shocked when they hear that the government gives away the airwaves free to the radio and the television conglomerates.

In an honest debate, the side that argued for the status quo as regards media wouldn't get 5 percent support. That's why we need to open up that honest debate. It won't be easy. But this book will help. You hold in your hands a key to unlocking the corporate media chains that have shackled real freedom of the press and real democracy in this country for all too long. Use it!

INTRODUCTION
BY SENATOR PAUL WELLSTONE, D-MINNESOTA

The media is not just any ordinary industry. It is the life blood of American democracy. We depend on the media for the free flow of information that enables citizens to participate in the democratic process. As James Madison wrote in 1822, "A popular government without popular information, or the means of acquiring it, is but a prologue to a farce or a tragedy, or perhaps both." That's why freedom of the press is enshrined in our Constitution. No other industry enjoys that kind of protection.

Yet, at the dawn of the 21st Century, America is experiencing a wave of media mergers and that is leading to an unprecedented concentration of ownership in the hands of a few giant communications firms. This rapid concentration of control over the U.S., and indeed global, media raises troubling questions for our system of representative democracy.

Over the past several years, I have expressed concern over the explosion of mergers in one industry after another, notably in agriculture and finance. But of all the industries where concentration of ownership is accelerating at such a rapid pace, it is consolidation in the media and entertainment industries that should alarm us most.

For our democracy to function effectively, we depend on the media to do two things. We depend on newspapers, radio, television and now the Internet to provide citizens with access to a wide and diverse range of opinions, analyses, and perspectives. And we depend on the media to hold concentrated power—whether public or private power—accountable to the people. The greater the diversity of ownership and control, the better media will be able to perform these vital functions.

But as ownership and control of the media becomes concentrated in the hands of fewer and fewer people, it becomes less likely that we can rely upon the media to fulfill these basic responsibilities. Common ownership and control is not conducive to diversity of viewpoints and perspectives. And as these far-flung multinational corporations extend their holdings and influence into more and more new industries—with interests of their own, as regards regulation in particular—how much confidence can we have that they will hold any of those interests accountable to the people?

Most Americans are shocked when they learn of the degree of media concentration that has occurred over the past 15 years. When Ben Bagdikian wrote *The Media Monopoly* back in 1983, about 50 media conglomerates controlled more than half of all broadcast media, newspapers, magazines, video, radio, music, publishing, and film in this country. By 1986, that number had shrunk from 50 to 29. By 1993 it had shrunk even further, to 20 firms. Today fewer than 10 multinational media conglomerates—Time Warner, Disney, Rupert Murdoch's NewsCorp, Viacom, Sony, Seagram, AT&T/Liberty Media, Bertelsmann, and GE—dominate most of the

American mass media landscape. The range and diversity of their holdings is astounding.

Growing consolidation of media corporations raises very urgent questions about political power in our democracy. As Gerald Levin, the chairman of Time Warner, said recently, global media is "fast becoming the predominant business of the 21st century," and it is therefore "more important than government. It's more important than educational institutions and non-profits."

Global media corporations wield enormous influence over the formulation of our public policy. Yet they often have direct economic stakes in the outcome of our public policy debates. And the larger they get, the more influence they exercise, the more money they can donate to members of Congress, and the more high-paid lobbyists they can afford to blanket the halls of Congress with their self-serving messages.

Ordinary citizens don't stand a chance of having their voices heard against the power and influence of these corporate titans. What's more, ordinary citizens have almost no say in the way these conglomerates operate. Yet, we know that what's good for global media corporations is not necessarily good for America.

So what, if anything, can we do about the crisis of concentration?

I believe that the media mergers that have led to this troubling degree of concentration warrant the highest level of scrutiny by our antitrust agencies and by the Federal Communications Commission (FCC). They may also require Congress to consider a new legislative framework to address the growing problem of media concentration. If our antitrust laws can't do anything to stop nine conglomerates from dominating this multi-trillion dollar industry, clearly we need to start rethinking our antitrust laws. I think it's long overdue for Congress and the White House to reassert the importance of antitrust laws in the global economy of the 21st century—and nowhere is such a move more urgently needed than in regard to the media industry.

Undoubtedly such an effort would meet considerable resistance, not least from media corporations themselves. Progress in the area of antitrust has almost always come in response to public pressure.

Yet, this is the fundamental quandary of democratic media reform: involvement of the public in this debate depends on coverage and attention by the major media that has traditionally been the source of information. Unfortunately, the record to date has not been encouraging. The major media have been virtually silent on the public policy implications of their own rapid consolidation over the past 15 years.

But, now, the silence is beginning to be broken. Citizens are beginning to ask tough questions about media mergers, and Bob McChesney and John Nichols are showing them how to turn those questions into a powerful movement for media reform.

Thanks to the courageous and groundbreaking work of tireless advocates such as McChesney and Nichols, more and more Americans are beginning to appreciate the enormity of the stakes involved in the debate over media concentration. And, with this book, citizens are being offered a sense of the power they have to force this issue onto the agenda of our political parties and, ultimately, of local, state, and federal government.

It is time for such a movement. Indeed, if we truly care about the health and future of American democracy, we must involve every citizen in this crucial work of insuring that the life blood of that democracy—information from diverse and distinct sources—is allowed to flow freely.

IT'S THE MEDIA, STUPID
BY JOHN NICHOLS & ROBERT W. MCCHESNEY

It was the rainiest, wettest, coldest April morning Washington had seen in a long time. And still they came—thousands of mostly young activists determined to mount a non-violent but noisy protest outside the spring 2000 meetings of the World Bank and the International Monetary Fund (IMF). As they reached a key intersection near the World Bank building, they were blocked by armed battalions of riot police and National Guardsmen. The authorities stood their ground, but the Mobilization for Global Justice activists refused to back down.

This was the sort of standoff to which even the most jaded television assignment editors dispatched their crews—despite the fact that the weather made for some fogged-up camera lenses. On the street, a reporter for one Washington television station pulled aside a young woman who was soaking wet, and announced to the cameraman that it was time to do a live shot. When the signal came that they were on air, the reporter started to make small talk with the activist about the miserable weather. "I really want to talk about the policies of the World Bank and the IMF," the young woman said. "Their structural adjustment policies are causing real harm in specific countries around the world..." The reporter pulled the microphone back, looked to the camera and said, "Well, everybody has an opinion. Let's go back to the anchor desk."

That same afternoon, as young people who had attended teach-ins, listened to debates and read literature and books in preparation for the demonstration continued to face down the police in the streets, conservative commentator Tony Snow was attacking the protesters on Washington radio as ignorant and uninformed. The next morning, The *Wall Street Journal* referred to them as "Global Village Idiots." The supposedly liberal *Washington Post* and *New York Times* editorial pages both dismissed the protests as not much more than a waste of police resources and everyone else's time. And, despite the fact that at least 150 activists were still in jail, and that people in Washington, across the nation and indeed, around the world, were buzzing about a new era of activism, television news programs went back to broadcasting the usual mix of commercials and vapid "news you can use."

Molly Ivins put it rather succinctly when she observed, a few days later, that "for reasons unclear to me, the mainstream media seem to have decided that anyone who questions any aspect of globalization is an extremist nut, despite the rather obvious fact that global poverty is growing under the kind auspices of the World Bank, the International Monetary Fund, and the World Trade Organization."

In our view, the reasons for this are clear. The closer a story gets to examining corporate power the less reliable our corporate media system is as a source of information that is useful to the citizens of a democracy. And on issues like the global capitalist economy, the corporate media are doubly unreliable, because they rank as perhaps the foremost beneficiaries of Wall Street–designed trade deals like NAFTA, and of the machinations of the three multilateral agencies developed to shape the global economy to serve corporate interests: the World Bank, the IMF and the World Trade Organization (WTO). Moreover, almost all the favored mainstream sources for coverage of global economic affairs are strident advocates for a corporate-driven vision of globalization. Thus, corporate journalists—even those low enough on the pecking order to be dispatched to stand in the rain on a Washington street corner—generally will find arguments against the status quo incomprehensible.

Just as the media dropped the ball in Washington in April, 2000, it blew a chance to cover an even more dramatic story of citizens speaking truth to power in the fall of 1999, when the WTO met in Seattle. As one of the most significant challenges to global economics in decades was playing out—a challenge so powerful that the WTO meetings were actually shut down for a time and ultimately failed to launch a new round of trade liberalization, a challenge so intense that President Clinton felt compelled to assert his agreement on a variety of issues with those protesting in the streets—the broadcast media treated the story as an event of secondary importance. There was no round-the-clock coverage, as was seen only four months earlier when John F. Kennedy Jr.'s fatal plane crash reshaped the broadcast schedules of CNN, the Fox News Channel, and every other cable TV news service for two full weeks. During the WTO meetings and demonstrations—which dealt with arguably the most important political issues of our age—

no attempt was made to provide comprehensive coverage. One night, as demonstrators filled the streets of Seattle and ministers of finance battled through the night over the most fundamental questions of how the global economy would be structured, as the President of the United States hunkered down in a hotel surrounded by armed troops, the Fox News Channel interrupted its scheduled programming for a live special report... not from Seattle, but from the scene of the latest doings of the parents of JonBenet Ramsey.

What happened in Seattle sums up the crisis for democracy that occurs when the media system is set up primarily to maximize profit for a handful of enormous self-interested corporations. An Orwellian disconnect is created. The news required for a functional democracy—the news that empowers citizens to act in their own interest and for the good of society—is discarded to make way for the trivial, sensational, and salacious. How many Americans have come home from a school board meeting, a city council session, a local demonstration or a mass national rally to discover the vital issues they had just addressed are being ignored or distorted? The flow of information that is the lifeblood of democracy is being choked by a media system that every day ignores a world of injustice and inequality, and the growing resistance to it.

No, the media system is not the sole cause of our political crisis, nor even the primary cause, but it reinforces every factor contributing to the crisis, and it fosters a climate in which the implementation of innovative democratic solutions is rendered all but impossible.

True, our media system is set up to serve the wealthy few, not the many, but it is within our power to change it. The point of this book is to let activists in on a secret that the manipulators of our politics have known for a long time. Political issues do not simply occur. They are made. And that's why, whether we as citizens, are talking about globalization, gun control, healthcare, prison reform, or labor, to shape our own issues and to affect change we need to access and alter the media. The purpose of this book is to assist in that process. Chapter 1 tackles media and our current crisis of democracy. Chapter 2 examines the rise of democratic media activism around the world in the 1990s. And Chapter 3 discusses current and future projects needed to establish a democratic media system in the United States.

Back in 1992, Bill Clinton's campaign strategists hung a sign in the war room of their Little Rock headquarters that read, "It's the economy, stupid." The point of the sign was to remind campaign workers to circle every discussion of election issues around to the subject of the sagging economy. In many senses, this book is like that sign. We are here to argue that it's time to point out the connections between media reform and democratic renewal. To sound a wake up call reminding us that access to communications is a non-negotiable demand in a democratic society, and that scoring real victories for labor, the environment, and social justice will be made all the more possible by opening up and democratizing the media. Meanwhile, when the corporate press comes looking for a soundbite on what the ruckus is all about, tell them, "It's the media, stupid."

Chapter 1
THE PROBLEM WITH THE U.S. MEDIA

"Media is not an issue, but that's because the media frame the topics of discussion—and, obviously, they're not going to put that on the list of issues that have to be discussed."—ALAN SCHROEDER

Americans devour media at a staggering rate; in 1999 the average American spent almost twelve hours per day with some form of media. We are also in the midst of an unprecedented technological revolution—based around digital technologies, typified by the Internet—that looks to weave media and electronic communication into nearly every waking moment of our lives. In conventional parlance, these developments are presented as benign; they are all about liberating individuals, investors, and consumers from the constraints of time and space while offering a cornucopia of exciting new options and possibilities. This, however, is a superficial and misleading perspective on what is happening. Indeed, when one lifts the hood, so to speak, to see what is driving the media revolution, a very different picture emerges. It is instead a world where highly concentrated corporate power is pulling the strings to dominate our existence so as to maximize return to shareholders, and to protect the corporation's role—and corporate power in general—from being subjected to the public scrutiny and political debate it so richly deserves. It is a poison pill for democracy.

Yet in our American democracy the issue of media barely registers. The structures of our media, the concentration of its ownership, the role that it plays in shaping the lives of our children, in commercializing our culture, and in warping our elections, has been off-limits. When we examine the reality of media in the year 2000, however, it becomes clear that this circumstance must shift. The case for making media an issue is made, above all, by a survey of the contemporary media landscape.

In 2000, the U.S. media system is dominated by fewer than ten transnational conglomerates: Disney, AOL–Time Warner, News Corporation, Viacom, Seagram (Universal), Sony, Liberty (AT&T), Bertelsmann, and General Electric (NBC). Their media revenues range from roughly $8 billion to $30 billion per year. These firms tend to have holdings in numerous media sectors. AOL–Time Warner, for example, ranks among the largest players in film production, recorded music, TV show production, cable TV channels, cable TV systems, book publishing, magazine publishing, and Internet service provision. The great profit in media today comes from taking a movie or TV show and milking it for maximum return through spin-off books, CDs, video games, and merchandise. Another twelve to fifteen firms, which do from $2 or $3 billion to $8 billion dollars per year in business, round out the system. These firms—like Comcast, Hearst, New York Times, Washington Post, Cox,

Advance, Tribune Company, Gannett—tend to be less developed conglomerates, focusing on only two or three media sectors. All in all, these two dozen or so firms control the overwhelming percentage of movies, TV shows, cable systems, cable channels, TV stations, radio stations, books, magazines, newspapers, billboards, music, and TV networks that constitute the media culture that occupies one-half of the average American's life. It is an extraordinary degree of economic and social power located in very few hands.[1]

It has not always been this way. Much of this concentration has taken place in the past few decades, as technology and market imperatives made concentration and conglomeration far more attractive and necessary. Today it is impossible for the small, independent firm to be anything but a marginal player in the industries mentioned above. Most important, the flames of media concentration were fanned by a collapsing commitment on the part of the federal government to serious antitrust prosecution, a diminution of the federal standards regarding fairness, and government "deregulation," most notably the 1996 Telecommunications Act. Congressional approval of the Telecommunications Act, after only a stilted and disengaged debate, was a historic turning point in media policy making in the United States, as it permitted a consolidation of media and communication ownership that had previously been unthinkable.

A surface survey of the statistics regarding media ownership, while deeply disturbing in what it reveals, fails to convey the full depth of the concentration of media ownership. Not only are media markets dominated by a handful of conglomerates with "barriers to entry," making it nearly impossible for newcomers to challenge their dominance, but they are also closely linked to each other in a manner that suggests almost a cartel-like arrangement. Some of the largest media firms own parts of the other giants; Liberty, for example, is the second largest shareholder in News Corporation and among the largest shareholders in AOL–Time Warner. Moreover, the media giants employ equity joint ventures—where two competing firms share ownership in a single venture—to an extent unknown almost anywhere else in the economy. These joint ventures work to reduce competition, lower risk, and increase profits. By 1999 the nine largest media giants had an equity joint venture with six, on average, of the other eight giants; often a media giant would have multiple joint ventures with another firm. In sum, this is a tightly knit community of owners, dominated by some of the wealthiest individuals in the world. Indeed, thirteen of the hundred wealthiest individuals in the world—all of whom are worth over $4 billion—are media magnates.[2]

Such concentration of media ownership is clearly negative by any standard that cherishes free speech and diversity in the marketplace of ideas. But concentration in media ownership is not the sole cause of the problems with the media, and in some cases it is not a significant factor at all. Concentration is important to a large extent because it magnifies the limitations of a commercial media system, and makes those limitations less susceptible to redress by the market. But this sounds very abstract, so let's cut to the bone: the problem with concentrated media is that it accentuates the two main problems of commercial media, hypercommercialism and denigration of public service. These are really two sides of the same coin. As massive media corporations are better able to commercially carpet bomb society, their ability or willingness to provide material with editorial and creative integrity declines. It is not that the individuals who run these firms are bad people; the problem is that they do destructive things by rationally following the market cues they are given. We have a media system set up to serve private investors first and foremost, not public citizens.

No better example of how this process works can be found than in the U.S. radio industry. Since deregulation of ownership in 1996, some one-half of U.S. stations have been sold. A few massive giants, owning hundreds of stations—as many as eight in each market—have come to dominate the industry. As profits shoot through the roof, low-budget standardized fare has nearly eliminated the local content, character, and creativity that were once features of this relatively inexpensive electronic medium. "A huge wave of consolidation has turned music stations into cash cows that focus on narrow playlists aimed at squeezing the most revenue from the richest demographics," the trade publication *Variety* observed in 1999. "Truth be told, in this era of megamergers, there has never been a greater need for a little diversity on the dial."[3]

The radio example points to the one other crucial group, aside from media owners, that gets treated with love and affection by corporate media executives: the corporate advertising community. Businesses spent some $214 billion in the United States on advertising in 1999—some 2.4 percent of the GDP—and almost all of this money ended up in the hands of some media firm.[4] Though journalists and civics teachers bristle at the notion, those media that depend upon advertising for the lion's share of their income—radio, TV, newspapers, magazines—are, in effect, part of the advertising industry. Throughout the 1990s the media giants used their market power to pummel their customers with ads and to bend over backward to make their media attractive to Madison Avenue. By 1999 the four major TV networks, for example, were providing nearly sixteen minutes per hour of commercials during prime time, an enormous increase from just a decade earlier.[5] A conglomerate like Time Warner was able to sign a $200 million advertising deal with General Motors that "crosses most of the entertainment company's divisions," so that "GM will have a first-look option on all automobile marketing opportunities within Warner Bros. operations."[6] Not content with traditional advertising, media firms are now working on "virtual ads," whereby "a marketer's product can be seamlessly inserted into live or taped broadcasts." With ads so inserted during actual programs, viewers will be unable to avoid the commercials through zapping.[7] Advertising has also been plugged into new venues, such as video games.[8] But this does not capture the full spread of commercialism. In television, for example, the new growth area for revenues is selling merchandise that is shown on its programs.[9] It barely caused a ripple when Tommy Hilfiger hired the Viacom-owned cable channel VH1, rather than an ad agency, to produce a series of TV ads, because VH1 is so effective at selling.[10] In sum, the entire U.S. media experience increasingly resembles an infomercial.

Nowhere is the commercial marination of the American mind more apparent than in the case of children, where the advertising assault was increased exponentially in the 1990s. There are now four full-time cable channels (owned by the four largest U.S. media firms) bombarding children with commercial programming twenty-four hours per day. Advertisers have targeted the youth market as arguably the most important in the nation. Girls between the ages of seven and fourteen spend some $24 billion per year and influence parental decisions worth another $66 billion. Commercial indoctrination of children is crucial to corporate America. One study revealed that when eight-year-olds were shown two pictures of identical shoes, one with the Nike logo and the other with the Kmart logo, they liked both equally. The response of twelve-year-olds was "Kmart, are you kidding me?"[11] This desire to indoctrinate fuels the commercial drive into education and suggests that the moral foundations for coming generations may be resting on a dubious base. Nobody knows what the exact consequence of this commercial blitzkrieg upon children will be, but the range of debate extends from "pretty bad" to "absolutely terrible." The only thing we know for certain is that the media giants and advertisers who prosper from it do not care and cannot care. It is outside their frame of reference.

In this light, it is worth considering the status of the long-standing conflict between "church and state" in media; this refers to the ability of journalists and creative workers to conduct their affairs without having output determined by what serves the immediate interests of advertisers, or owners for that matter. In conventional wisdom, the U.S. media system has been at its best when the divider between "church and state"—especially though not exclusively in journalism—has been pronounced and respected. That way media users can regard the articles and news and entertainment programs they read, see, and hear in the media as reflecting the best judgment of media workers, not the surreptitious bribe of a commercial interest. Nowhere has the collapse of editorial integrity been more pronounced than in magazine publishing. As the late Alexander Liberman, legendary editorial director of Condé Nast, noted in 1999, advertisers "have too much power. They determine, if not specifically, then generally what magazines are now."[12] A series of scandals in the late 1990s affirmed what has been suspected: Advertisers have tremendous control over the editorial copy in U.S. magazines, and editors who are discomfited by this had best find employment elsewhere. "They're glitz bags," Norman Mailer said of magazines in 1999. "They are so obviously driven by the ads that the ads take prominence over the stories."[13]

Hollywood films have so thoroughly embraced commercial values that *Variety* now writes of the "burgeoning subfield of Product Placement Cinema."[14] Conglomerate control of films and music and television (all of the TV networks, all of the main studios but the floundering MGM, and all four of the firms that dominate the U.S. music scene are owned by the eight largest media firms) has opened the floodgates to commercialism and has proven deadly for creativity. "A movie studio is part of this huge corporate cocoon," Peter Bart, editor of *Variety* and former head of Paramount, writes, "and therefore, theoretically, a studio should be willing to take bigger risks because one bad movie ... won't erode the value of the [parent company's] shares. But the way it works out, the studios are if anything more risk averse. They are desperate to hedge their bets. It's the nature of bureaucratic self-protection.... The pressure is reflected in the sort of movies that get made... the sort of pablum that studios chewed on for ten years, that's gone through endless rewrites, has been pretested by endless focus groups, and is successful—if insipid."[15] Or as an executive at Time Warner's "independent" studio New Line Pictures puts it, "We're very marketing-driven as a company. I'm instructed not to greenlight a project if I can't articulate how to sell it."[16] As Bart concludes, this is "not exactly a recipe for art."

This said, we are not attempting to make a blanket indictment of everything produced by the corporate media system. We are not suggesting that every article or broadcast segment is foul, nor that they are all tainted, nor even that some material that is tainted cannot also be good. There are extremely talented people employed in the commercial media system, and the pressure to satisfy audiences does indeed sometimes promote excellent fare. But corporate and commercial pressures greatly undermine the overall quality of the system and skew it in ways that are not at all the result of audience demand. In the world of corporate media, the key is to attract the preferred target audience while spending as little money as possible. In the battle for consumer attention, this strongly promotes a rehashing of tried-and-true formulae, as well as the use of sex, violence, and what is termed "shock" or "gross-out" fare. In a world where people are surrounded by innumerable media options (albeit owned by numerable firms), sex and violence are proven attention getters.[17]

Corporate control and hypercommercialism are having what may be their most devastating effects in the realm of journalism. There is no need to romanticize the nature of U.S. professional journalism from the middle of the century into the 1980s; in many respects it was deeply flawed. Yet whatever autonomy and integrity journalism enjoyed during that time of Bob Woodward, Carl Bernstein, and *Lou Grant* is now under sustained and unyielding attack by corporate owners in the hunt for profit. No more striking evidence for this exists than the results of a 1999 Pew Research Center poll of journalists concerning their profession. Until the 1990s, journalists tended to be stalwart defenders of the media system, and most scholarship emphasized journalists' hypersensitivity to criticism of their field. No more. The Pew poll found that "at both the local and national level, majorities of working journalists say the increased bottom-line pressure is hurting the quality of coverage."[18] "This past year," David Halberstam wrote in 1999, "has been, I think, the worst year for American journalism since I entered the profession forty-four years ago."[19] Bob Woodward, the Watergate investigator who has enjoyed one of the most successful and prestigious media careers of the era, says that in these days of hypercommercialism and hypercompetition, "No one is the keeper of the conscience of journalism."[20]

The brave new world of corporate journalism manifests itself in many ways. The primary effects of tightened corporate control are a serious reduction in staff, combined with pressure to do vastly less expensive and less controversial lifestyle and feature stories. Where there is "news," it often takes the form of canned crime reports that foster unrealistic and unnecessary fears. This is the magic elixir for the bottom line.[21] Sometimes the new world of corporate journalism is typified by blatant corporate censorship of stories that might hurt the image of the media owner. But the maniacal media baron as portrayed in James Bond films or profiles of Rupert Murdoch is far less a danger than the cautious and compromised editor who seeks to "balance" a responsibility to readers or viewers with a duty to serve his boss and the advertisers. In media today, even among journalists who entered the field for the noblest of reasons, there is an internalized bias to simply shy away from controversial journalism that might enmesh a media firm in a battle with powerful corporations or government agencies. True, such conflicts have always been the stuff of great journalism, but they can make for very bad business, and in the current climate business trumps journalism just about every time.

The most common and noticeable effect of the corporate noose on journalism is that it simply allows commercial values to redirect journalism to its most profitable position. So it is that relatively vast resources are deployed for news pitched at a narrow business class, and suited to their needs and prejudices; it is predominant in newspapers, magazines, and television.[22] Likewise, news for the masses increasingly consists of stories about celebrities, royal families, athletes, natural disasters, plane crashes, and train wrecks. Political coverage is limited to regurgitating what some politician says, and "good" journalism is practiced when a politician from the other side of the aisle is given a chance to respond. But that is not journalism; it is stenography. Perhaps the strongest indictment of corporate journalism is that the preponderance of it would be compatible with an authoritarian political regime. So it is that China has few qualms about letting most commercial news from the United States inside its borders; it can see that this low caliber of journalism is hardly a threat to its rule. It is the BBC, with its regrettable penchant for covering politics seriously, that draws the commissar's ire.

There is also intense pressure for journalism to contribute immediately and directly to the bottom line. One Tennessee TV station received adverse publicity for offering to do TV news "puff pieces" on local businesses in exchange for $15,000 payments. It is important to note, however, that the mistake made by that Tennessee station was not the spirit of the offer—it well reflects the pattern across the news media—but, rather, the baldness of it.[23] Firms also use the news to hype their other programming, as in 1996 when *NBC Nightly News* made the Summer Olympics its most covered news story that year, even though none of the other networks had the Olympics ranked on their top-ten lists. Why? Because NBC was airing the Olympics that summer—and reaping the attendant financial rewards. The fall of 1999 saw a huge debate erupt in newspaper circles after the *Los Angeles Times* devoted the entire editorial space in an edition of its 164-page Sunday magazine to articles, photos and graphics describing downtown Los Angeles' new Staples Center sports arena. The newspaper did not reveal at the time of the magazine's publication, however, that it would be dividing the $2 million in revenues generated by the section with the owners of the arena. So dark was the scenario that the former publisher of the *L.A. Times*, Otis Chandler, sent a letter to the staff describing the new management's move as "unbelievably stupid and unprofessional."[24]

Above all, however, the *L.A. Times* was blatant. It allowed the corrupting linkage between advertisers and the media to be clearly identified. More often than not, a measure of subtlety keeps controversies under wraps.

In addition to triviality and craven commercialism, the willingness or capacity of U.S. journalism to challenge elite assumptions or to question the status quo—never especially great in the best of times—has shriveled. So it was, for example, that the preponderance of media coverage of the 1999 war in Kosovo lamely reflected elite opinion in the United States, when even the rudimentary application of traditional journalism standards would point to severe discrepancies in the official story line.[25]

All told, this creates a crisis for democracy. Alexis de Tocqueville rightly celebrated the role that a free and diverse media plays not only in greasing the wheels of electoral systems but in maintaining the very structures of civil society. The nineteenth-century surveyor of the American public landscape went so far as to say of news organizations, "They maintain civilization."[26] Who would seriously attempt to make such a statement about today's media?

This caliber of journalism is decidedly unsatisfactory for a democratic society. Democratic journalism should provide a ruthless accounting of the powers-that-be and the powers-that-want-to-be, both in government and politics and in the extremely powerful corporate sector. Democratic journalism should also provide background information and a full range of viewpoints on the main social and political issues of the day. We cannot expect each news medium to provide all of these elements of a quality journalism, but in combination, a democratic media system should make this caliber of journalism readily available to the entire population. It may be true that the media are not primarily responsible for the apathy, cynicism, and depoliticization that mark U.S. electoral politics today; in fact, media executives use this lack of interest in politics sometimes to justify their declining attention to public affairs and their continuing coverage of trivial and mindless stories. But it is also true that the lack of journalism has fanned the flames of depoliticization and contributed to U.S. electoral politics becoming increasingly a commercial contest sponsored by a small group of billionaires, for which most Americans rationally assume they have no role to play, or stake in the outcome. Presidential elections, which now draw less than half of the electorate to the polls, have become media entertainments, complete with graphics and play-by-play reports but bereft of any suggestion that citizens should—or could—actually play any more of a role in this extravaganza than they do in the Super Bowl or the Academy Awards.

Not only is political coverage in American media increasingly empty and meaningless, there is also less and less of it. Indeed, while the amount of air time allotted the Super Bowl and the Academy Awards has increased in recent years—as prices paid for properly placed advertising skyrockets—coverage of the most fundamental workings of our democracy is getting squeezed. And without apology. Asked by the *Dallas Morning News* about slackening coverage of the 2000 presidential campaign by America's television networks, former ABC White House correspondent Sam Donaldson answered, "We are doing a very minimal amount of coverage at ABC. Outside of *Nightline* and our Sunday show, ABC News, in my opinion, has simply forfeited the field." But don't let's pick on

ABC; all the broadcast networks are cutting back, according to the watchdog group Alliance for Better Campaigns. During the 2000 presidential primary season, the Alliance reported, the networks were giving the presidential campaign 20 percent less coverage than they did in 1988—the last time the U.S. saw serious contests for the Democratic and Republican presidential nominations. CNN president Rick Kaplan told the *Philadelphia Inquirer* that the major broadcast networks had been "derelict" in their coverage of the 2000 campaign. "They're making their news divisions less important than they were. They're just getting out." Is it any wonder that serious analysts predict that the November 2000 presidential contest could draw one of the lowest voter turnouts in the nation's history? There are plenty of culprits to blame for declining voter participation. But we cannot help but believe any discussion of declining voter participation that fails to address declining network coverage of the politics should be interrupted with a hearty bellow of, "It's the media, stupid!"

In years past this criticism of the U.S. media would have been met by howls of indignation from journalists, professors, and citizens of every stripe. Ours was a truly free press, they would argue, celebrating the majesty of the freedom in American history. Today that response is muted; the asininity and degradation of our media culture is palpable and hard to digest even for the old true believers. Or, perhaps, especially for the old true believers—who have seen their faith in what the good media might do erased by the reality of what it does. Yet the system still has many who defend it, albeit with less enthusiasm and righteous fervor than in years gone by. One defense is that the media system is based on the pursuit of profit, so firms are compelled to "give the people what they want," or face economic ruin. There is an element of truth to this claim, but it should not be exaggerated. Media markets are hardly competitive in an economic sense, and because of that firms have a great deal more power to force people to choose from what they deem most profitable. Moreover, media markets often are set up with advertisers, not people, as the primary target; in such cases the needs of the citizenry fade from view beneath the commercial imperatives of Madison Avenue. This is especially true in the newspaper industry, where the drive to attract upmarket readers has led in many cities to a radical decline in serious coverage of poor and working-class neighborhoods as resources are shifted to the coverage of suburban areas where the readers that advertisers want tend to congregate. Moreover, even a purely competitive market media system, and one without any advertising, would be far from perfect. Markets are predicated upon one dollar, one vote, rather than one person, one vote. Hence rich individuals have many more votes than people who are poor. The market in this sense is more plutocratic than democratic. While the market can play an important role in a democratic media system, it should never comprise the entirety of a democratic media system.

Another defense of the existing order is that this is the "natural" American system; if someone is dissatisfied with it, that person should shut up or move to another country, preferably on the other side of the world. The "love-it-or-leave-it" theory, aggressively advanced by the likes of millionaire radio personality Rush Limbaugh, holds that the First Amendment to the U.S. Constitution has authorized two dozen profit-seeking transnational corporations to rule U.S. media with ample government subsidies but with no public "interference" otherwise. This is an argument that does not stand up to any historical scrutiny. It is true that the First Amendment prohibits congressional interference with a free press; but it does not therefore authorize concentrated corporate and advertiser domination of the press. Imagine a parallel phenomenon in the practice of religion: If a handful of faiths were using their accumulated resources and their lobbying influence with government to gain dominance in the spiritual life of the land while forcing faiths with different ideas and values out of the public sphere, would First Amendment absolutists argue that this was the intent of the "freedom of religion" protection? If they tried to do so, they would be stymied by the courts, laughed out of any serious debate, and appropriately labeled as self-serving theocratic totalitarians.

The First Amendment belongs to all Americans, not just the billionaire investors in a handful of giant media firms, and it is based on the notion that democracy demands a press that serves us all. We are not arguing for government censorship of the commercial media—in fact, we oppose efforts in that direction—but we think efforts to reduce the power of Wall Street and Madison Avenue, and to increase the role of Main Street and every other sector of the population, in the running of our media system are entirely consistent with the meaning of the First Amendment.

It is worth noting that there is nothing "natural" about the existing media system. The system is the result of government laws and regulations that have made it possible for massive private concerns to play such a significant role in our media's affairs. These laws—like the Telecommunications Act of 1996—are usually written by and for the media firms with almost no public participation. There is rarely any press coverage of the important debates leading up to enactment of these laws, except in the business and trade press where it is covered as an issue of importance to investors, not as an issue of consequence for citizens. The only debate occurs when different media firms or corporate sectors square off against each other. (That is why they need such huge lobbying arsenals.) In addition, these media firms hardly operate in some mythical free market; they receive lavish subsidies such as the gift of scarce radio-TV spectrum (valued at well over $100 billion) for which they pay not one penny.

We believe, as we will argue in Chapter 3, that the public should not merely dole out corporate welfare to transnational media conglomerates; it should prudently devise a system of subsidies to encourage the growth of a viable nonprofit and noncommercial media sector, as well as a sector of small commercially owned media. The one tangible attempt at publicly supported media—public radio and television—has been underfunded and hamstrung since the outset. It is arguable that America has not yet begun to explore the possibilities of noncommercial broadcasting as a healthy alternative to commercial media and as a balm for a failing democracy. We believe, therefore, that any viable program of media reform requires a supercharged noncommercial public radio and TV system.

Some also defend the corporate media status quo by asserting that the media do not have much effect upon anyone, so this is much ado about nothing. This perspective holds that media consumers are savvy in the ways of the media, and can interpret commercial messages critically. It's true that few citizens swallow everything the media serves up hook, line, and sinker. In the old Soviet Union, few citizens believed what they read in *Pravda* or *Izvestia*, but that didn't mean the society would not have been well served by massive reform of the media system. And to suggest that the corporate media have no effect upon us seems to be untenable; after all, there are limits to what we can expect citizens to "read into" media messages. Nor do we suggest that all that media produces should be met with deep skepticism; we recognize that the system offers much material that is useful and entertaining. Our claim is simply that the media system produces vastly less of quality than it would if corporate and commercial pressures were lessened.

There is one new argument in defense of the media status quo, the argument that the Internet will set us free. Ironically, it seems that the same people (like George Gilder) who just a few years ago were telling us how great the media system was in the United States are now suddenly conceding that it is, indeed, dreadful, but that there is no reason for concern. The Internet, they tell us, allows us to escape this failed media landscape. How? The theory goes something like this: Because anyone can start a website at a relatively nominal expense, and because anyone online can access any website, then the giant media firms are dinosaurs from another age and their monopoly control surely must be doomed once the Internet comet smashes into the earth. Happy days are here again. Heaven on earth. Digital nirvana. "Free at last, free at last, thanks to the Internet we are free at last," one can almost hear the techno-enthusiasts chirping. And all we have to do is sit back, wrap our mitts around our mouse, and let the private sector do its thing. It doesn't get any easier or better than that, does it?

As with the other defenses of the media status quo, there is an important element of truth, or half-truth, in this euphoric vision of the Internet as a magical technology. The Internet, and digital communication more broadly, is radically changing our lives. In a few years the world we live in is going to look quite different from the world of just a few years ago. Moreover, the Internet is forcing a reconfiguration of the media industries, as the shift to digital communication means that the traditional distinctions between media and even communication sectors are disappearing. So it is that the most immediate consequence of the digital revolution is convergence, whereby telephone companies like AT&T and computer companies like Microsoft become active in digital media. But ironically, this convergence has not led to a burst of competition so much as it has led to unprecedented corporate consolidation in and among the media, telecommunication, and computer industries. In 1996 there were seven regional telephone companies and eleven U.S. telecom giants overall. Today there are six, and each has a massive war chest of additional media and telecommunication interests. AT&T is now the nation's largest cable company. At this point, it looks as if the corporate media quasi-cartel is evolving into a corporate communication quasi-cartel. Microsoft, for example, has used its colossal riches to purchase outright or to grab stakes in scores of media, cable, and telecommunication companies across the globe. That way, however the Internet develops, Microsoft will be in a position not only to profit from it but to be dominant in it.

Specifically, the hope that the Internet is going to overturn the media system and open up massive space for new voices, not to mention marginal, dissident, or noncommercial voices, has been proven to be unfounded. This does not mean that there will not be an exciting and important use of the Internet by activist and noncommercial interests, only that such a use of an Internet ruled by commercial values will quickly get pushed to the margins, as has been the case. The core problem with the notion in the first place was that it mistook the existing power of the media giants as being based on technology, when in fact that power is also based on the market. While it is true that anyone can start a website, it has proven nearly impossible for anyone to start a commercially viable website unless they are owned by or affiliated with an existing media giant. Indeed, by the end of 1999, the evidence suggested that the Internet was going to enhance concentration among media firms, as well as their overall size.[27] One survey found that far from being "a democratizing force, allowing a large number of relatively equal market contestants to compete on a level playing field," the Internet instead gave the dominant sites "an accelerating advantage over their competitors."[28] Even Microsoft, with its billions of dollars in hard cash, effectively abandoned producing content for the Internet after squandering a few hundred million dollars on the endeavor in the late 1990s.

When AOL purchased Time Warner in January 2000 it all too forcefully proved that the Internet will not spawn a new generation of commercially viable media companies. After all, for the roughly $100 billion that AOL valued Time Warner, it could produce vastly more media content than Time Warner produces, and flood the Internet with new media content. Instead, AOL spent its money buying Time Warner's market power, which it knew was nearly priceless.

The explanation is simple: the media giants have several tremendous advantages as they colonize the Internet. They have existing digital programming to put on the web, while it is exceedingly expensive for new competitors to produce such fare. The giants to bring their advertisers over to their websites as part of their contracts with their traditional media. They can heavily publicize their web activities over their traditional media, in a manner that would be cost prohibitive for any Internet media start-up that did not have a traditional media outlet. The media giants also have tremendous leverage with Internet service providers, search engines, and portals to get premier position on the screen. And, to top it off, the media giants have invested heavily in Internet content ventures to keep a finger in the pie. The media firms know that their ultimate survival depends upon their dominating cyberspace, so they are willing to assume losses there far longer than would any rational investor without media holdings.[29] In combination, these factors are overwhelming. Moreover, as cyberspace is colonized by the media giants, it appears to be fanning the flames of hypercommercialism inherent in the traditional media system. Media websites often feature e-commerce as a means of generating revenues, and, to attract advertisers, the crumbling notion of editorial integrity from commercial pressure has been compromised even further.[30] More broadly, evidence suggests that the Internet, so far, has been far more a source for aggravating social inequality in the United States than for arresting it.[31]

More concentration of media ownership than ever. Declining standards of journalism. Hypercommercialized culture and entertainment. A declining civic life and a collapsing democracy. And no hope on the Internet. Depressing, no?

And that's not the half of it. The system seems almost impervious to change. Consider how powerful the media and communication lobbies are in Washington, D.C., as they routinely use the campaign contribution scalpel to remove politicians' backbones. By virtually every measure, the corporate media, telecommunication and computer lobbies, and trade associations are among the most powerful in the nation.[32] The corporate media not only have piles of money but also control access to the public, something that politicians covet. In 1999 the National Association of Broadcasters, the trade association of the commercial broadcasters, went so far as to use the wives of members of Congress in their televised public service announcements. As one report noted, "It is a quiet way of further ingratiating itself with lawmakers."[33] Finally, the corporate media are in the position of being able to provide the press coverage of any debates over media policy and hence to define what the public will be exposed to on the issues. "Media is not an issue, but that's because the media frame the topics of discussion—and, obviously, they're not going to put that on the list of issues that have to be discussed," says Alan Schroeder, author of the recent book, *Presidential Debates: Forty Years of High-Risk TV* (Columbia University Press).[34] This trump card ought to make the corporate media the envy of the corporate community.

But there are grounds for optimism. Incessant hyper-commercialism and lowest-common-denominator journalism have eliminated much of the enthusiasm for the corporate media system, as we mentioned above. Recent polling suggests that the people "get it" when it comes to media issues. They are concerned, even angry, and they strongly favor a political and governmental response to the problem—as opposed to continued reliance on an essentially unregulated free market. A 1995 survey by Citizens Research for the Center for Media Education found that 55 percent of those polled felt commercial television had a negative impact on children, while only 29 percent saw it as a positive. Overwhelmingly, the survey respondents felt that commercial interests were to blame for poor-quality television—with 41 percent laying the blame squarely at the doorstep of the broadcast networks, while 27 percent pointed to advertisers; only 16 percent said quality was poor because that was what consumers wanted. In the same survey, 82 percent of those interviewed expressed concern that commercial broadcast television was providing too little educational programming for children, and more than 80 percent of those surveyed said that they felt stronger regulation of broadcasting by the government was necessary to address concerns about the impact television has on young people.[35]

A comfort level with strong governmental regulation of broadcast media is a constant in survey research regarding media issues. A May 1999 survey by Lake Snell Perry & Associates for the advocacy group People for Better Television found that 80 percent of those queried favored a requirement that broadcasters meet greater public service obligations, particularly in the areas of local and children's programming. The same survey found 72 percent support for making children's television programming commercial-free, while 85 percent favored development of more educational programming aimed at adults. A full 79 percent of those surveyed endorsed a proposal that commercial broadcasters be required to pay 5 percent of their revenues into a fund for development of noncommercial, public-service-oriented programming.[36]

Polling evidence also suggests that people increasingly see corporate media as an antidemocratic agency. The Pew Research Center for the People and the Press regularly studies public attitudes toward the media in general, with a special focus on questions that measure perceptions regarding parallels between the values of citizens and the values of the media. In 1985, 54 percent of Americans described the media as "moral," while 13 percent chose the term "immoral." In 1999 only 40 percent said the media was moral, while 38 percent said it was immoral.[37] In 1995, 54 percent of citizens surveyed by Pew said media "helps democracy," while only 23 percent described it as "hurting democracy." In 1999, the number saying media helps democracy had dropped to 45 percent, while the number identifying media as harmful to democracy had risen to 38 percent.[38]

These polls are hardly the final word on the subject, but they seem to confirm what the authors have noted in their own experiences: there is an openness to candid and frank discussions about media that would have been unthinkable even a decade ago. We have something to build upon, to organize around. But that point notwithstanding, there is still no serious debate on the subject on Capitol Hill. When U.S. Sen. Paul Wellstone, D-Minn., called for strong congressional action to address media ownership issues following the October 1999 announcement of the CBS-Viacom merger plan, he essentially stood alone.

It doesn't have to be this way. Public policy could effectively restructure our media system such that it has a significant and viable nonprofit and noncommercial component. Once media is made a bona fide political issue, as soon as it is "in play," the forces favoring media reform will prevail. We may not get everything we want, but we will get a lot of what we want. (That is why the media giants work so incessantly to ensure that media issues never see the light of day.) So getting media reform on the public agenda is the first and greatest obstacle we face. And here we run up against the ultimate defense of the media status quo, after all the other arguments have been discredited. This is the notion that there is simply no other way for media to be operated in a democratic society, so it is not even an issue worth considering. Any change from the status quo must be, by definition, a change for the worse. This is a powerful and paralyzing notion, and it carries considerable weight in the United States, not only for media reform but for social reform in general. But by looking outside the United States we can see the fraudulent nature of this claim, for it is in these other lands that democratic forces are mobilizing to oppose the sort of hypercommercial, concentrated corporate media system we have in the United States. The lessons from abroad provide a powerful sense of how Americans can—and, we would argue, must—creatively and constructively approach media reform in the United States.

Chapter 2
GLOBAL MEDIA AND ITS DISCONTENTS

"Broadcasting is too important to the functioning of a democracy for decisions to be left entirely to the broadcasters."—TONY BENN

Campaigning across New Zealand in anticipation of that country's November 1999 parliamentary elections, Jim Anderton, the head of a feisty young political grouping known as the Alliance Party, devoted a substantial portion of his time on the trail to discussions of the media. Unlike politicians in the United States, for whom talk of "media" immediately boils down to a question of whether to go with commercials of the 30- or 60-second variety, the veteran parliamentarian was talking about the media as an issue in the campaign. At press conferences and in speeches, Anderton—who several years ago was rated in a poll as the politician New Zealanders would most like to see as their prime minister, and who leads a party that after the November elections joined New Zealand's governing coalition—laid out a vision for how the Alliance proposed to take on the giants of global media in order to provide New Zealanders with radically different, and radically better, broadcast and print media.[1] "Over the past decade we have treated broadcasting as primarily a commercial activity. That perspective is ill conceived and naive," declared the platform on which Anderton campaigned. "Broadcasting is a much more complex activity than this, comprising technologies, social and cultural practices, cultural forms, a set of industries in its own right, and dynamic institutionalized forms which are continuously evolving. But above all it is an idea. This idea is that a society's broadcasting media, as the most important of all communications enterprises, should serve the public interest."[2]

Reaffirming a vision that the airwaves are public property, and arguing that the government must take responsibility for policing and regulating that public property, Anderton called for a radical restructuring of New Zealand's broadcasting: limiting foreign ownership of television and radio stations, developing new government-funded television and radio networks and stations to serve minority communities, elimination of all forms of advertising during hours when children view television to combat "intrusive and cynical manipulations through commercial messages," and massively increased support for and funding of existing public-sector broadcasting. "We do not believe that private media are essentially interested in New Zealand popular cultural expression, nor is it reasonable to expect them to be beyond a certain regulated level," explained the Alliance leader's policy declaration. "It is therefore essential that significant broadcasting organizations in both radio and television should remain in public ownership."[3]

The determination of Anderton and the Alliance to

make media an issue in what for the party was a critical campaign serves as a powerful illustration of how the crisis for democracy that results from the corporate domination of media is not merely a U.S. phenomenon. It is instructive, too, that the Alliance in combination with the Greens and the Labour Party won a majority of the votes in the November 1999 elections, throwing out of power a business-dominated government. When we look at what is happening to media abroad, we see a growing willingness on the part of democratic forces to organize for media reforms that challenge the patterns of globalization and corporate domination. These calls for media reform are also proving popular with voters, if not with the business class. In this chapter we outline the nature of the emerging global commercial media system, and the contours of the democratic resistance to it. We believe that there are hopeful and powerfully instructive lessons for Americans in these global developments.

But first, let's look at the developments to which movements for media reform are responding. Since the 1980s, a global commercial media market has developed. As a result of deregulation of national media markets, new communication technologies, and heavy pressure from the U.S. government and the international business community, the face of media has undergone striking change in virtually every country on the planet. Whereas media systems were formerly best understood as national phenomena, with a minor role played by media imports, today it is more appropriate to regard media as a global system with national variants.

The global media system is the province of some seventy or eighty firms that provide the vast majority of the world's media fare. There are two distinct tiers to this hierarchy. The first tier is comprised of eight transnational media conglomerates (AOL–Time Warner, Disney, Bertelsmann, News Corporation, Viacom, Sony, AT&T, and Vivendi Universal) that all collect between $10 billion and $30 billion per year in annual media-related revenues. These firms tend to be dominant players in numerous media sectors and to do business all across the world. The remaining sixty or seventy firms are smaller, tend to concentrate more upon one or two media sectors, and are more likely to be national or regional powerhouses. A great chasm separates the first tier media firms and those near the bottom of the second tier. AOL–Time Warner, for example, will do some $35 billion in business in 2000; a firm near the bottom like Spain's domestic giant Sogecable will do around $700 million.[4]

The transnational media giants, as one leading media analyst notes, "are increasingly setting their sights on global expansion."[5] In 1999, for example, Disney completely reorganized its corporate structure to expand and strengthen its "global presence."[6] Disney's enthusiasm is understandable; experts project that the major Hollywood studios, which currently earn around one-half of their income outside the United States, will see that portion rise to two-thirds in the next five to ten years.[7] An examination of the top ten grossing films in each of the eight largest national markets after the United States in the summer of 1999 reveals that Hollywood films, each produced by a first-tier media giant, accounted for seventy of them.[8]

But the global media system should not be perceived as one where U.S.-based transnational conglomerates dump their standard fare on new audiences. On the contrary, the media giants localize their content whenever feasible, and almost always enter new markets in a partnership with local firms and investors. Sony's Hollywood-based studios have been most aggressive in producing films and localized TV content, doing so across Europe, Latin America, and Asia.[9] Rupert Murdoch's News Corp., however, is the flagship firm for establishing major joint ventures with local firms across the globe, especially with regard to cable and satellite television.[10] By 1999, even India's massive domestic film industry had been penetrated by joint ventures with News Corp.'s Fox studios and several other Hollywood giants.[11]

The balance of the largest media firms are meeting the challenge and going global with a vengeance. AT&T's Liberty Media and Microsoft have both made major investments in global cable systems.[12] Even second-tier global media firms find it necessary to move beyond their national or regional markets in order to grow—and to avoid being taken over by more aggressive competitors.

Nor is this pattern of global growth and concentration exclusive to the largest, mostly U.S.-based firms. Deregulation of national media ownership restrictions has both opened up national markets to outsiders and permitted domestic giants to grow ever more powerful. Spanish media and telecommunication firms, for example, "are invading Latin America in search of its corporate treasures."[13] Major national media markets like Mexico, Brazil, and India are each increasingly dominated by just a few massive media firms, and these firms all work closely in joint ventures with the transnational media giants. In no sense can the massive capitalist media firms of the developing world like Mexico's *Tele-*

visa or Brazil's *Globo* be characterized as "oppositional" to the global corporate media system; they are integral players in that system.

This is not just a process taking place in what has been called the Third World. In Britain, the television and newspaper industries have undergone a tremendous consolidation in recent years, and U.S.-based firms are now prominent players in these oligopolistic markets.[14] Indeed, most nations have vastly more concentrated ownership of media than the United States, if only due to their smaller populations and geographic sizes. And the process is far from over.

The European Union, for example, is working to help European media firms become not only regional, but global, powers.[15] As a result of deregulation, the *New York Times* observed that "Europe's television industry is suddenly in the grip of an American-style consolidation."[16] In addition to first-tier media giants like News Corp. and Bertelsmann, European TV is falling into the hands of a few regional giants like Canal Plus, SBS, Fininvest, and Kirch. These firms hope to use their European base as the foundation for eventual expansion into the United States, either directly or through joint ventures.[17]

One other development is working hand in hand with global media concentration: the rise of a highly concentrated global advertising industry. For the past decade the advertising agency industry has consolidated at a rate even greater than that of the media industry, and is now dominated by three to six global giants that dwarf the remaining players. These giants tend to have subsidiaries in every major market, and they increasingly represent corporate clients who need global marketing campaigns.[18] These ad agency titans find that the global media giants are best positioned to provide them with the global reach their clients need and demand.

So far what we have presented in this chapter may not be widely known, but it is hardly controversial. The pages of business and trade publications teem with this information on a daily basis. And were we to leave the discussion at this point, investors might be the only audience with a direct interest in the subject. But we are not discussing the widget market here, or some other incidental commercial undertaking. We are discussing the means of communication and information distribution—the lifeblood of journalism and culture—and, accordingly, the foundation of democracy. As we discussed regarding the media giants in chapter 1, the most striking way to conceive of the negative implications of the global commercial media market is quite simple: As the power of the largest firms grows, they use that power to commercialize content to the greatest extent possible and, if necessary, to protect their political interests, and they denigrate any notion of public service that might interfere with either of those aims.

This attack on public service assumes many forms. Deregulation and the rise of the commercial media market have cast the future of public service broadcasting in grave jeopardy. Traditional public service broadcasters, such as the British Broadcasting Corporation (BBC), have begun to look like square pegs in a world of round holes. They are increasingly pressured to adopt the practices of commercial firms in order to establish their efficiency and worth, but as they go commercial they lose their *raison d'être*. They even get chastised for being publicly subsidized competitors to the now dominant commercial media.[19] The *Economist* calls this the "conundrum" of public-service broadcasting: "If it goes upmarket, nobody watches it, so it is hard to justify state finance. If it goes downmarket, it ceases to look like public-service broadcasting, so it is hard to justify state finance."[20] There is a crucial change assumed in that formulation, however. At its best, public broadcasters sought to provide high-quality, noncommercial fare to the entire population regardless of what the commercial media were doing. This made it possible for them to develop mass audiences while providing noncommercial standards. In this new era where corporate media giants ride roughshod over governments, public service broadcasters are expected to concede popular programming to commercial interests, and to concentrate upon that for which there is not much of a market. A vicious cycle is created, wherein underfunded public broadcasting outlets are unable to compete for viewers, are told to turn to commercial support, and ultimately are threatened with privatization.

Until public broadcasters are again provided with the resources and mandate to provide noncommercial programming to large audiences, they are on a dead-end street. They may survive as quasi-commercial entities, but they will not survive as genuine public service broadcasters. An example from New Zealand is illustrative. After the government sold off most of Radio New Zealand's stations to private investors, complaints began to arise that the system's respected newsgathering operation was too costly to maintain. The Catch-22 situation was summed up by the Alliance Party's Jim Anderton: "Radio New Zealand News is under pressure for the simple reason that it is not supplying news to anyone other than Radio NZ. It is effectively a single radio station trying to support a nationwide network of newsrooms. No wonder it's in a squeeze."[21]

The defense of public broadcasting—and its reformation along less bureaucratic lines—is one of the cornerstones of media reform movements worldwide. There is a growing sense that we are on the verge of losing a unique and indispensable cultural resource. It is a concern well expressed by an Australian senator during a debate over funding the Australian Broadcasting Corporation: "Starving the ABC of its funds means that the ABC cannot afford to purchase the rights to a whole spectrum of content, including sport, and especially cannot afford to produce its own content."[22]

As in the United States, a striking and important consequence of the global commercial media market has been the attack on journalism, and the reduction in its capacity to serve as the basis for an informed, participating citizenry. Let us be clear here: we are not blaming the global media system for all the flaws in journalism. Establishing a media system that fosters a free-wheeling, independent, wide-ranging, and vibrant journalism and political culture is no easy matter, though it is something that all democratic societies should aspire to develop. National press systems prior to—and in conjunction with—the global commercial system were and are sometimes adequate at this job, but many were failures. Frequently, the media have been owned by wealthy individuals or firms that have clearly censored journalism to support their usually reactionary politics, as is the case in Turkey today.[23] Both public and commercial broadcasters in many nations have often been handmaidens of the dominant political parties and interests. In places like Mexico, Peru, and Brazil, the dominant commercial broadcasters have tended to be in bed with the dominant probusiness political parties, and to use their media power aggressively and shamelessly to maintain the favored parties in power.[24] Editors and reporters from dissident media who courageously bucked the system and reported on those in power have often found themselves arrested or on the receiving end of a beating or a gunshot. These practices continue today across the world.[25]

In theory the rise of the global media giants was regarded as a plus to many countries; these organizations, it was thought, would use their money, power, and prestige to bring neutral, professional, nonpartisan journalism to nations desperate for such fare. And, indeed, to the extent "globalization" affects national media regulation to undermine censorship of the news, that is a good thing.[26] The sad truth, however, is that the caliber of the journalism provided by these giants tends to be deplorable. When a journalist actually attempts to maintain a higher standard, she quickly learns that she does not fit into the new media landscape. Award-winning writer Robert Fisk was until 1986 the Middle East correspondent for the *Times* of London. He left, he says, because of the quality of journalism—or is it lack of quality?—demanded by *Times* owner Rupert Murdoch. "I would not accept the Murdoch ethos. Over and over again, I was writing against the paper's presumptions. I was in the odd situation where the *Times* didn't want me to leave but they would find themselves embarrassed at the content of what I wrote. The *Times* is an example of what has happened to much [of] journalism in Britain and Europe, which has become dominated by the micro-journalism of television and radio newscasts of one minute each."[27]

It should come as no surprise, then, that reporters and editors connected to the media giants are almost never the ones who show up as the arrested and murdered reporters on the annual list published by the Committee to Protect Journalists.[28] The media giants are not interested in pursuing dangerous stories that cost a lot of time and money to pursue, promise little financial payoff, and can antagonize governmental authorities with whom the media barons desperately want to stay on good terms. Most indicative of this trend has been the manner in which four of the five largest media firms in the world have fallen over themselves attempting to please the government of China. Disney's and News Corp.'s campaign to please the Chinese rulers by watering down their journalism and operations has been chronicled elsewhere.[29] Time Warner and Viacom entered the fray in the fall of 1999. What these episodes make clear is that no viable system of journalism can be expected from a system under the thumb of massive self-interested commercial organizations.

The most visible manifestation of the rise of the global commercial media has been not its journalism but its broader popular consumer culture, as its fare is drenched in advertising and commercialism. Report after report chronicles the rapid and stunning shift in culture, especially among middle- and upper-class youth, across the world as the commercial media system subsumes each nation's television system.[30] Although there is considerable debate over whether this is a "U.S. invasion" or a broader corporate invasion, or whether this is good or bad, there is little debate over one point. This is a generation that is under pressure from the media it consumes to be brazenly materialistic, selfish, depoliticized and non-socially minded. To the extent one finds these values problematic for a democracy, we all should be concerned.[31] The commercial media system is the ideological linchpin of the globalizing market economy. Consider the case of the Czech Republic. Only a decade ago the young generation led the "Velvet Revolution" against the communist regime under the slogan "Truth and love must prevail over lies and hatred." Ten years later even the *Wall Street Journal* acknowledged that the Czech Republic had turned into a demoralized morass, where "an unnerving dash to the free market" had created a society awash with greed, selfishness, corruption, and scams.[32]

If we may generalize, the type of political culture that accompanies the rise of the corporate media system worldwide looks to be increasingly like that found in the United States: in the place of informed debate or political parties organizing along the full spectrum of opinion, there will be vacuous journalism and elections, dominated by public relations, big money, moronic political advertising and limited debate on tangible issues. It is a world where the market and commercial values overwhelm notions of democracy and civic culture, a world where depoliticization runs rampant, and a world where the wealthy few face fewer and fewer threats of political challenge.

Some argue that this critique of the global media system is premature, and that we must wait for the other shoe to hit the floor. When the Internet matures, the argument in the United States and other lands goes, it will set us free. When people can easily get on line and access websites from around the world, the power of the media giants and the global advertisers to dominate journalism and culture will diminish, if not be eliminated. Already, dissidents have used new media to rouse support in places like China, Mexico, Saudi Arabia and Indonesia. In 1998, activists used the Internet to generate widespread opposition to the embryonic Multilateral Agreement on Investments, an issue that was getting short shrift in the corporate media. Organizers of the fall 1999 protests against the WTO in Seattle made extensive use of the Internet. And, it is notable that some of the wisest critiques of contemporary media, such as the British Campaign for Press and Broadcast Freedom's "21st Century Media" document, are readily available online.[33]

Yet while it is true that the Internet is changing much about our lives, and some of the changes will be for the better, the notion that it will slay the global corporate media system lacks evidence and strains credulity. What we discussed in Chapter 1 regarding the Internet in the United States is true as well for the entire world. To date the commercially driven Internet is increasingly dominated by large corporate concerns, and commercialism permeates their actions in cyberspace every bit as much, if not more, than in their traditional realms. The largest media, telecommunication, and computer firms are racing to establish global "self-regulation" for the Internet, so that once they figure out how to maximize profit from the web, they can keep governments from messing with their goose that is laying golden eggs.[34] What an ironic—or tragic—fate for a medium that only exists as a result of 25 years of lavish public sector investment. It is particularly tragic at the global level, where studies acknowledge that a commercially driven Internet will greatly polarize most societies along "have" and "have not" lines, especially in the less wealthy nations.[35] It does not have to be this way, but to alter its course will require a firm public commitment to establish a healthy and viable nonprofit and noncommercial sector to the Internet. That will not happen if the matter is left to market forces.

Many people around the world are not waiting for a mythic technology to free them; they are organizing to reform their media systems to better serve the democratic needs of the great mass of citizens. These movements are many and they are varied. Yet, all share basic values regarding media. They understand that the corporate media system is in many respects the advancing army of a global economic system that is hell bent on producing profits regardless of the social and environmental implications. This global "free market" economic system has produced considerable benefits for some (usually very wealthy) people, and notable benefits for many more (usually the middle and upper middle classes), but it has come at a very high cost. Social inequality is increasing in nearly every nation, as is the divide between rich nations and poor nations.[36] For working class and poor people, especially women, the results of the global "free market" can be disastrous.[37]

Because of the obvious linkages between the corporate media system and the global economic system, media reform is seen by a growing number of activists around the world as a necessary part of any democratic political platform; rarely is it seen anymore as a "single issue" reform activity. In country after country, media reform is being integrated into the platforms, the campaigns and the parliamentary initiatives of political parties that refuse any longer to operate in denial of the role that media plays in a democracy. This is absolutely essential for success; although media activism can and must assume many forms, it is when that activism is advanced by political parties and related mass movements that media reform can most effectively be linked to broader issues of social justice. This, of course, is the fundamental step that is required for the development of the broad-based support necessary for success. The importance of political parties as vehicles for pushing media reform issues into the public discourse is arguably the single most vital lesson from abroad for Americans to learn concerning media reform.

It would, of course, be unduly romantic to suggest that the development of the global commercial media market has been paralleled by a political response of equally definitional force. Challenges to monopoly and commercialization have yet to reach critical mass in any nation, let alone on an international scale that might cause the media giants to tremble—as, for instance, the campaign against genetic modification of food has caused multinational conglomerates such as Monsanto to quake in recent years.[38] Indeed, one of the great tragedies as regards media activism is that, as the processes of globalization, conglomeration, and commercialization sped up in the early 1990s, many traditional parties of the left abandoned the critiques of commercial media that had, historically, been among their core values.[39]

Take as an example the British Labour Party. Throughout much of its history, the Labour party was an explicitly socialist grouping that nurtured a healthy skepticism regarding media giants within Great Britain and beyond its borders. Targeted for trashing by "the Tory press" from its earliest days, the party displayed little caution in proposing tough controls on media monopoly, and campaigning for a strong, publicly-funded broadcasting authority.[40] It also showed a penchant for direct-action on the newsstands. On and off during its early history, the Labour party published its own mass-circulation daily newspaper, *The Daily Herald*, which like the German Social Democrats' *Vorwarts* and the French Socialists' *L'Humanite* competed directly and at times quite successfully with publications owned by the press barons.[41] In the 1970s and 1980s, Labour cabinet ministers such as Tony Benn were in the forefront of a brief flurry of serious discussion about the role that the government might play in guaranteeing ideological diversity in print and broadcast media. Benn recalls sparking an intense national debate in the 1970s by declaring that "broadcasting is too important to the functioning of a democracy for decisions to be left entirely to the broadcasters." Benn's battle cry resonated with Labour party activists and media watchdogs who developed Britain's innovative Campaign for Press and Broadcast Freedom in 1979.[42] Through the 1980s, the Labour party maintained an openness to the proposals of the Campaign for Press and Broadcast Freedom, which emphasized the need for strengthening the BBC, diversifying ownership of broadcast and print media, and challenging the supremacy of media conglomerates. As late as 1992, the Labour party continued to advocate for what by American standards would be considered radical reform of the media landscape. Its 1992 campaign platform contained a lengthy section on "The Media"—tucked between statements on "Ethnic Minorities" and "The European Community"—which stated: "Labour wants a wider choice for listeners and readers in the broadcast and printed media. Promoting greater diversity and tackling concentration of ownership will ensure wider choice." That commitment was followed by specific proposals for full funding of the BBC, development of monopoly controls to prevent concentration of ownership of newspapers and broadcast outlets and a host of other plans.[43]

As the 1990s wore on, however, Labour became increasingly comfortable with big media. The political rise of Tony Blair and his "New Labour" allies saw the party that once decried corporate media as little more than a vehicle for recounting "the frivolous doings of the idle rich"[44] move to the right of the Conservative Party of Margaret Thatcher and John Major on media issues. Labour's abandonment of its traditional stance created such a "topsy-turvy affair," according to British journalists Dan Glaister and Andrew Culf, that in 1996, "a Conservative government laid down a 20 percent threshold restricting newspaper groups from diversifying into television, while Labour united with right-wing Tory rebels to scrap the limits altogether."[45] Effectively, Labour became the defender of media conglomeration and monopoly. Around the same time, Blair flew to Australia to meet with Rupert Murdoch, who soon after switched his mass-circulation *Sun* newspaper from an ardently Thatcherite Conservativism to a position of fervent support for Blair's "New Labour." By 1999, Blair was carrying Murdoch's water, using his role as British PM to advance Murdoch's business ambitions in both Italy and China.[46]

Some of Labour's savviest media critics—who are, not

coincidentally, among the party's strongest critics of corporate excess—are leaving it altogether. Ken Livingstone, a Labour member of parliament who was denied the party's nomination for mayor of London despite winning overwhelming support from party members, jumped ship to run a independent campaign for the capital city's top job in the spring of 2000. Freed of the party whip, Livingstone conducted an epic campaign that spoke bluntly about media monopoly and other ills. Livingstone argued that the party under Blair's leadership was not merely losing touch with its values—it was surrendering its ability to offer a realistic response to issues of globalization that were fundamentally altering people's lives. Livingstone's message resonated. He won a landslide victory, and took charge of a new city government that included three Greens who had been elected on a platform that highlighted support for expanding democracy by, among other things, supporting greater media diversity.

Labour's shift is merely one stark illustration of a collapse of principle on the part of many—though not all—traditional social democratic parties around the world. "At the precise moment when socialist parties should have been mounting a powerful challenge to the media conglomerates and the monopoly control that is taking over our politics, our culture and every aspect of our lives, the leaders of these parties were sitting down with the CEOs and saying, 'We can do more for you than Thatcher and the conservatives did,'" says Benn, who has watched with mounting frustration as, in his words, "Blair has steered this old bus (the Labour party) completely off course."[47]

With the rise of the Blair-generated "Third Way"

ideology—characterized by its advocacy for market "solutions," free trade and a diminished governmental role in regulation of the economy in general and corporations in particular—the old parties of the left have for the most part abandoned their commitment to challenging private media monopolies and to using governmental policies and spending to promote the sort of ideologically diverse media that sustains democracy. Germany's Gerhard Schroeder and a host of other leaders of social democratic parties have joined leaders of historically liberal parties, such as the American Democrats and the Canadian Liberals, in embracing a neo-liberal, market-driven, corporation-defined, privatizing vision of government that Gregor Gysi, leader of Germany's rapidly growing Party of Democratic Socialism, accurately describes as an "unhistoric" politics in which "social justice and ecological sustainability are strangers."[48] "The old-line parties have abandoned the playing field. They have stopped fighting for social and economic justice, choosing instead to seek the favor of the corporations the people want them to be battling," says Svend Robinson, a New Democratic Party member of the Canadian parliament. "I don't know if there is anyplace where this is more evident than in battles over media monopoly, corporate conglomeration and foreign control of our media."[49]

As the old parties have made their peace with markets, corporate capital, globalization of the economy and the media that these patterns produce, they have left a void. In country after country, that void is being filled by new political groupings that, as part of a broader critique of neoliberalism, are making noise about the dangers posed to democracy by corporatization of the discourse. Just as Green parties—many of which have embraced media reform proposals—forced nations to look anew at questions of environmental protection and sustainability in the 1980s, so these new-line parties are forcing media issues onto the agenda. "This is an issue that's emerging all over the world. It's a huge concern. People are genuinely alarmed that at the same time we're witnessing growing concentration of ownership of media we're also seeing massive cuts in publicly owned media. It's a double whammy," says Canada's Robinson. "This neo-liberal, right-wing takeover of the media is something that people are aware of, and they don't like it. But the old-line parties aren't willing to address the issue. This is what is going to distinguish new-line parties all over the world—a willingness to talk frankly about issues of media control and to propose an alternative to what's happening. It's inevitable. After you've had somebody say to you for the thousandth time, 'How come we never hear about these issues in the media,' you start to realize that the media itself is the issue."[50]

Robinson describes the groups that are mounting a political response to the development of the global media market and its devastating impact on democracy and the lives of citizens as "new-line parties," and this distinction is important. Americans in particular need to recognize that the image we generally hold of political parties—as nothing more than election machines that are more interested in collecting campaign money than in giving voice to citizens, shaping the debate or creating a politics of meaning—is not universally admired or accepted. While it is true that Blair, Schroeder, Israel's Ehud Barak, and others have done yeoman's work to

"Americanize" parties in other states—even going so far as to import Bill Clinton's pollsters and consultants—the homogenization of politics has met with significant opposition in many lands.[51] That opposition has given rise to new parties or, particularly in former Soviet-bloc states, to radically reshaped old parties. These parties are far more in touch with grassroots anger regarding the media, and with the movements that have arisen to give voice to that anger. Following recent electoral advances for his party in Berlin and eastern Germany at the expense of Schroeder's Social Democrats, the Party of Democratic Socialism's Gysi explained, "The Social Democrats are only used to reacting to pressure from the right. But now they have to react to pressure from the left as well. It is normal in many other countries, and they have to get used to the idea of it being normal here too."[52]

A number of the parties that have taken the most aggressive stances regarding media issues—as part of broader programs that challenge corporate conglomeration and market-driven globalization—refer to themselves as members of "The Third Left." The name is intended to suggest an advancement from the narrowly focused political or economic critiques historically associated with pre-Marxist and orthodox Marxist movements toward an approach that comfortably links feminist, green and traditional left values in a new model of politics.[54] Critical to the message of these red-green groupings around the world is a determination to present a clear vision of the more humane, sustainable, and functional society that these parties would use political power to develop. "We work for a society in which all people have equal worth and the same right to a good life,' declares the program of Sweden's Left party, which has experienced a steady growth in its electoral strength as opinion polling has identified the party as that country's third most popular political grouping. "We want to live in a world where people solve conflicts by peaceful means and live in harmony with nature. In community and cooperation a living culture is created which strengthens people's identity and self-esteem and provides society valuable inspiration and criticism."[54]

In neighboring Finland, a 10-year-old Third-Left party, the Left Alliance is now a member of the governing coalition, holding 20 parliamentary seats and two cabinet posts. Like the Left Party, the Left Alliance promotes a radical vision based on core values of freedom, democracy and socially and ecologically sustainable development. "In order for real freedom to be realized, society and its constituent parts must be democratic," its platform declares. "A democratic society is characterized by the fact that freedom and civil rights are not based on ownership or social position, but on the recognition of the human dignity of all people. In a democratic society all individuals have an equal and continuing opportunity to develop, study, work and influence irrespective of their social, linguistic, cultural or ethnic background. Real freedom for everyone is only achieved through the strong position and political guidance of democratically elected decision-makers as a counterweight to the market-oriented economic power."[55]

An awareness of the relationship between ideologically diverse media and real democracy is a constant among third-left parties, as well as the green, non-socialist left, and even non-left wing groupings that have begun to embrace media issues in countries around the world. "From the point of view of democracy, it is essential that all political decision-making is preceded by a genuine and interactive discussion in which all interested parties and even temporary coalitions are openly and impartially heard. In addition to political decision-making, essential economic decisions should also be as public as possible," argues the Finnish Left Alliance platform. "The openness and public nature of decision-making can only be guaranteed with the aid of free, pluralistic and diversified communications. In an open society, communications must go in all directions, which is why we need the possibility of interactive communications in addition to the mass media. In a democratic society the freedom of communication and the diversity of the media represent in principle a positive direction in development, because the fragmentation of the media and the public gives people a wider freedom and choice than before. Advanced information technology offers increasing possibilities for contacts and interaction between people and different NGOs. In a world of diversifying media, society ensures that ownership is not excessively concentrated, and that diversity and variability as well as the accessibility of the media and public communication services are supported by taxes wherever necessary."[56]

Sweden's Left party has made media reform central to its politics, emphasizing at every turn that "Prerequisites for democracy are freedom of speech and press freedom..."[57] and arguing that "in a living democracy it is necessary to have a broad and independent choice of media. Everyone should be able to express their opinions in one form or another. All opinions should be able to reach the public."[58] The Left party pushes aggressive and innovative media reforms, including abolition of all advertising on radio and television and a program of subsidies for print media designed to guarantee that democracy is enriched by the broad availability of publications expressing distinct and sometimes unpopular views.[59] The party, which in 1998 national elections saw its vote double to 12 percent of the total, does not simply talk about big ideas and grand visions, however. It has joined with labor groups to boycott a television station that refused to honor a Swedish law barring the airing of advertisements aimed directly at children, it has developed sophisticated newspapers, magazines, and websites to advance its ideas, and its members have been active players in the creation of radio programming designed to serve Sweden's growing immigrant community, women, and young people.[60]

Sweden's experience with the Left Party and the ban on TV advertising to children points to an important lesson: Once the left gets media reform in play, the traditional parties can no longer serve the interests of the corporate media with abandon. Moreover, media reform is an issue that has appeal across the political spectrum. Most of Sweden's parties now support the ban on TV advertising to children—it is popular with voters—and, in fact, Sweden intends to push to make the ban universal for the 15 EU nations when it assumes the rotating presidency of the EU in 2001. It looks to be a defining battle in the campaign for media reform.[61] Already Greece and Norway have enacted similar bans, and Denmark is contemplating doing so as well.

The coalition building that is at the heart of these evolving parties—like the fall 1999 anti–World Trade Organization protests in Seattle and the spring 2000 anti-

IMF and World Bank protests in Washington—recalls popular front models of the 1930s. In refreshing contrast to traditional liberal parties, "inside-outside" approaches characterize their challenge to global media. No longer do party strategists and "consultants" form policy positions in isolation. Parties of the left and even of the center, which are raising media issues, have seen their positions informed by the ground-breaking work of media unions, watchdog groups, academics, and grassroots activists, who have often had a hard time getting a hearing from old-line parties. Frequently, the activists find that newer, less bureaucratic and more politically open parties are enthusiastic about incorporating media issues into their agenda.[62] Thus, in Brazil, media activists found an easy ally in the Workers Party of Luis Inacio Lula Da Silva, which used its powerful grassroots networks to organize demonstrations outside the headquarters of Brazilian media conglomerates that the activists identified as having failed to provide serious coverage of the political process in that country.[63] In the new political dynamic of post-apartheid South Africa, the comprehensive stance on broadcasting policy advanced by the Congress of South Africa Trade Unionists (COSATU) and media unions affiliated with it has influenced the approach not only of the African National Congress and the South African Communist Party, with which the unions have long maintained close ties, but also of smaller parties that range across the political spectrum. During the debate over South Africa's 1998 Broadcasting Bill, COSATU proposed dozens of specific amendments, many of which ultimately were accepted.[64]

In contrast to COSATU's ability to influence the

somewhat more open political process in South Africa, some of the ablest union and media activists in the world still struggle to get a hearing from old-line parties that have given up on fighting for democratic control over the global commercial media market or, worse yet, actually support policies that encourage monopoly, cross-ownership, foreign control of media, and commercialization. In Great Britain, for instance, the leadership of the Labour party distanced itself in the mid-1990s from the Campaign for Press and Broadcast Freedom (CPBF), which—with the Press Trust of India—has come up with some of the most innovative policy proposals yet advanced for the development of a diverse, democracy sustaining media. The campaign's response, in anticipation of the 1997 British elections, was to publish a political manifesto, or platform, of its own.[65] That manifesto opens with this declaration:

"The contours of media in the next millennium—what we see, hear, and read, how we receive it, who owns and controls it, and how we pay for it—are not minor issues for political parties. Indeed, to the extent that changes in our society make us ever more reliant on the media for information and entertainment, they are becoming more pervasive and powerful in shaping our responses to the actual political, social, and cultural changes we are experiencing.

"The CPBF's concern is that debates about media policy, certainly over the past decade, have been firmly directed and influenced by a range of media corporations and lobbying groups whose primary focus has been to ensure policies favorable to their commercial success and growth. Also, the main political parties have accepted that media companies should be encouraged to expand to take advantage of the 'multimedia revolution' and compete with the global media giants like Time Warner and Walt Disney.

"The voices of ordinary viewers and listeners, those working in the media, and those concerned about the democratic and cultural importance of the media have been neglected. It is time now for our voices and arguments to have wider impact and influence..."[66]

The manifesto, one of the most impressive documents yet produced by the global movement for media reform, had an unexpected impact. While Labour leaders took tea with Murdoch and other media kingpins, the British Liberal Democrat party wrote a platform that prominently featured several proposals developed by the Campaign for Press and Broadcast Freedom. Traditionally a centrist group that struggled on the periphery of the process, the Liberal Democrats scored their best showing in the post–World War II era in the 1997 elections. That strong performance at the polls was credited, at least in part, to the willingness of Liberal Democrats to address issues, such as globalization of the economy, genetic modification of food and media monopoly, over which the old Labour party would once have claimed ownership.[67]

In New Zealand and Australia, relatively new political parties have worked closely with unions and activists to make media an issue—with dramatic and instructive results. Jim Anderton's Alliance party, which was formed in 1991 as a coalition of greens, Maori rights campaigners and refugees from the Labour party, which was drifting from its socialist moorings, has become a home even for frustrated former journalists. After a 19-year career in broadcasting in New Zealand and Australia, which culminated in her appearing from

1987 to 1996 as host of a popular national talk show on Radio Pacific and the Newstalk ZB networks, Pam Corkery stepped away from the microphone and into the political fight over media. Elected to the New Zealand parliament on the Alliance slate in 1996, she became the party's spokesperson on communications, information technology and arts and culture. Corkery's experience in radio, television and print media, along with her passionate opposition to privatization of public broadcasting services marked her as the parliament's most effective advocate on media issues. She used her platform to campaign with an energy and a focus that shook up the debate in that country—even forcing the Labour party to rethink its movement toward neoliberal positions on privatization and broadcast policy.[68]

Early on in her parliamentary career, Corkery declared the fight to assert popular control over the media to be "at the very least, a human rights issue." Working with Anderton and other Alliance leaders, Corkery has helped to build a powerful "inside-outside" movement that has seen the Alliance raise issues of media monopoly on the floor of the parliament and on the streets of Auckland, Wellington, and Christchurch with unions, Maori and Pacific islander organizations, and grassroots media activists. In particular, this coalition has dogged Tony O'Reilly, the former Heinz Soup executive who began building a media empire in Ireland and has now extended it to South Africa, New Zealand, and other countries. After purchasing *The Auckland Herald* newspaper, O'Reilly began to gobble up recently privatized radio stations—laying off staff, cutting news operations and threatening to break a deal to have the privatized stations buy news from Radio New Zealand. The storm that the Alliance and New Zealand's media unions raised over the question of whether one man should control so much of a small nation's media led to hearings, debates, and investigations. It reopened the whole question of privatization and, eventually, prompted leaders of the Labour party to indicate that they would oppose any further media privatizations.[69]

Working closely with unions representing beleaguered Radio New Zealand workers, the Alliance has defended the public system's highly-regarded news gathering operations—the Kiwi equivalent of National Public Radio news in the U.S. When leaders of the conservative National Party, which lead the governing coalition at the time, complained about the cost of maintaining Radio New Zealand's news operations in the spring of 1999, Anderton angrily replied that costs were a factor only because the government had sold off huge portions of the Radio New Zealand network to private interests and had then failed to position the Radio New Zealand news operations to sell news to the new private stations—effectively creating a no-win situation for independent news gathering in the country. Attacking the National Party–appointed board of Radio New Zealand for its pro-privatization stances, Anderton declared, "The entire board should be sacked and replaced with professionals who understand the radio industry, and who don't have a vested interest in carving it up for their own profit."[70]

Not satisfied merely to defend the public broadcasting sector, the Alliance has begun to work with media unions, indigenous peoples, artists, academics and activists to develop proposals to reshape media in New

Zealand. In the fall of 1999, as the party campaigned in national elections where it would win a strong showing, its leaders issued a platform which promised an Alliance government would:

➤Set "Kiwi quotas" on free-to-air radio and television, establishing a minimum of 30 percent local content for television and 15 percent for music radio. The regulations would include sub-quotas designed to encourage the development of particular types of programming, in order to maintain balance and quality, and to steer production money to New Zealand's indigenous artists. In announcing the plan, Alliance Party deputy leader Sandra Lee declared, "It is the responsibility of any government to ensure that New Zealanders have the opportunities to be creative and to excel in the arts if they choose. As a nation, we must then be able to share in our successes. That may mean the right to watch free-to-air sporting events or the possibility to choose to watch and listen to quality New Zealand programs."[71]

➤Establish a Youth Radio Network, in response to proposals championed by New Zealand music star Neil Finn and modeled along the lines of a similar network in Australia. "Radio is one of the most important influences on young lives," explained Anderton. "Young people are as entitled as other groups to have the choice of a dedicated commercial free radio network available to them. Surveys have revealed a widespread demand for the choice not only for music but for the chance for young people to hear their own news, current affairs, comedy, drama and even talkback."[72]

➤Create and fully fund radio and television broadcast networks and programming designed to serve ethnic minorities, and restore Radio New Zealand International in order to provide service to remote islands in the South Pacific where a growing portion of New Zealand's immigrant population has roots.

➤Implement rules designed to eliminate television advertising during programs viewed by school-age children—a move that would extend existing protections for younger children. "We protect pre-schoolers, but primary-age children also deserve protection from commercial bombardment because they haven't fully developed skills to be able to distinguish commercials from programs," says Anderton. "Children have the right to be fully informed and entertained without being subjected to intrusive and cynical manipulation by commercial messages."[73]

The New Zealand model for building coalitions around media issues and then taking those issues to the heart of the political debate has strong parallels in Australia, where a small but energetic party known as the Australian Democrats has developed perhaps the most sophisticated political response yet seen to concentration of media ownership, domestic content issues, monopoly and commercialism.

The Australian Democrats are not a traditional party of the left, nor would they fit comfortably into the Third-Left category occupied by Sweden's Left Party, Finland's Left Alliance or Iceland's Alliance. Yet, they certainly meet the "new-line party" standard established by Canada's Svend Robinson. Founded in 1977 as a reform party with a strong environmentalist bent, the Australian Democrats made a name for themselves especially among young voters by taking tough stands in support of environmental protection, nuclear disarmament, aboriginal rights at home and human rights abroad. In the 1990s, the party has emerged as a solid supporter of sustainable development and a determined watchdog over Australian media. Working closely with the national "Save the ABC" movement, which was developed by media unions and consumers to oppose privatization proposals and funding cuts designed to undermine the Australian Broadcasting Corporation, the Australian Democrats became the most outspoken parliamentary defenders of that nation's popular yet embattled public broadcasting service.

Though they remain a small party, the Australian Democrats have registered significant victories in fights over the structure of media in their country. In 1997, working with unions and media activists nationwide, the Australian Democrats succeeded in convincing the government to abandon proposals that would have weakened existing limits on media cross-ownership by domestic and foreign conglomerates. Their work in conjunction with "Save the ABC" activists forced the government to scrap plans to restructure public broadcasting in a manner that would have meant cuts in services. And they gained support for the establishment of a federal government inquiry into patterns of media ownership.[74] By the spring of 2000, the Australian Democrats were leading the fight to provide government funding for development of ABC's on-line and digital television projects. The goal, the Democrats explained, was to assure that ABC is not forced into commercial arrangements with private concerns that might seek to dilute its independence and profit from its good name.

Legislative victories are only one test of the Australian Democrats' success, however. The real measure of their impact may well come in the shifting of attitudes toward media issues within Australia. By making media a central focus of their national campaigns and by forcing debates on subjects such as media ownership, foreign content on television, digital technology, and related issues, the Australian Democrats have pushed media issues into the political debate and—in what may be their greatest triumph—onto the front pages. For instance, appointments to the Australian Broadcasting Corporation Board are no longer the perfunctory distribution of political plums that they once were; not with the Australian Democrats using each new round of appointments to raise questions of political favoritism, backdoor deals and special-interest influence.[75]

Senator Vicki Bourne, a 10-year veteran of the country's upper house of government who serves as the Australian Democrats spokesperson on communications, has worked with some success to redefine the debate over ABC funding from one of where to make cuts to one of how service can be expanded. In a typically impassioned address to the Senate on March 31, 1999, Bourne placed the defense of public-sector broadcasting at the heart of the debate over media diversity. "We are talking about diversity of content and diversity of ownership at a time when the (government) is doing everything (it) can to nobble, to cripple, to decimate and to destroy the ABC," Bourne declared. "The ABC is Australia's real provider of broadcast diversity. The ABC broadcasts content free from commercial pressure and in so doing is able to deliver content which appeals to a wide cross-section of the community... In rural communities it is the ABC which provides diversity, it is the ABC which provides local content, it is the ABC which provides a broadcasting service that the metropolitan commercial free-to-air broadcasters continue to believe is not commercially viable."[76]

Then, Bourne offered a glimpse of what might be the future of media activism in a political context. She spoke bluntly about the failure of private media conglomerates to provide a full picture of the world—a picture that ultimately is necessary if citizens in a democracy are to be able to play a meaningful role in setting policies regarding foreign entanglements. "In Europe, the crisis in Kosovo is being filmed and reported by Australians employed by ABC," Bourne told the Senate. "I cannot help but notice the difference in broadcasts from other networks who do not have people on the ground there. Relying on overseas broadcasts is simply not good enough; it is just not the same. Despite globalization, we still require news and current affairs reports to be broadcast into our lounge rooms by our own voices—voices who know and understand how these important issues affect our communities..."[77] A human rights campaigner for close to a quarter century, Bourne argues that only with a diverse and independent media will Australians be able to obtain the information, the ideas and the sense of perspective necessary to perform their duties as citizens."There can be no doubt that a strong and independent ABC is absolutely and utterly in the best interest of Australians," Bourne declared in 1998. "In fact, it is vital to our democracy."[78]

The notion that a diverse and independent media is vital to democracy is not new. But it has too rarely been expressed on a regular basis in the corridors of political and governmental power. Once the issue is raised, however, the debate shifts. Suddenly, questions that seem technical, obscure, complex, or inconsequential take on a new meaning. No longer are citizens willing to cede to industry lobbyists and their political pawns control of the debate over ownership of the means by which a democracy discusses fundamental questions.

So says Bharati Ray, a former top administrator of the University of Calcutta, who now serves in the upper chamber of the Indian Parliament. Over lunch in her modest quarters near the great governmental buildings of Delhi, she listened with open delight to a review of the evidence of mounting media activism and its embrace by parties of the left. One of the most articulate advocates for the Indian left, which has a long history of raising concerns about foreign ownership of media, print and broadcast monopolies, and commercialization, she was genuinely pleased to learn that issues that concerned her and so many Indians were being raised in other lands.

But then Ray scowled. "Why are we unaware of these developments?" she asked. "Why do we not know more of this activity?" Ray knew the answer, of course. She was well aware that few reports on international media activism are featured on the evening news. Yet, the veteran teacher was not accepting excuses. "We must begin immediately to discuss what is being done around the world. We must come together. We must hear what others are doing so that we may imitate them. We must tell others what we are doing so that they may imitate us," she said. "Once we all begin to realize that we are not working in isolation, that we are a part of a great response to globalization, I think that the potential for the forces of democracy to succeed will be very great indeed."[79]

Indeed.

Chapter 3
MAKING MEDIA AN ISSUE IN AMERICAN POLITICS

"I always tell people: You can't separate a desire for more democracy from a willingness to get involved in media work."—KAREN KUBBY

On a windblown February night in 1992, more than 400 people tramped through the blustery streets of Keene, New Hampshire, to fill a hall at the local state college. They had come to hear Ralph Nader inform them that the American democracy their New England forebears pledged their lives and fortunes to initiate had degenerated to a perilous place. They had come, as well, to hear Nader's prescription for curing the ails of the body politic. In an address that kept the audience riveted for the better part of two hours, Nader ably described the flaws in the political culture: "issueless politics" practiced by candidates so compromised as to be "beyond redemption," "celluloid campaigning," "an increasingly and not surprisingly disengaged electorate."[1] In America, Nader told the crowd, "political campaigns are tedious, insubstantial, posturing, practiced gestures." For voters faced with choices between the likes of Bill Clinton and Paul Tsongas, Nader's description of the symptoms of a declining democracy came as no great surprise. Yet, his prescription for how to cure the condition was unexpected. The nation's most respected consumer activist mentioned some predictable remedies—public financing of campaigns, electoral reforms, even a "none-of-the-above" ballot option to allow frustrated electors an out—but he devoted much of his energy to proposing media reforms designed to sustain and encourage genuine democracy.

"We, the citizens, own the airwaves, yet we don't control them. The corporations that control them feed us a steady diet of electronic junk food and it is making our democracy sick," Nader declared. "What would happen if citizens controlled their own broadcast networks? What would happen if the purpose of television and radio was to provide people with the information they need to participate fully in our democracy—rather than simply to be consumers?"[2]

Nader was running a faux presidential campaign designed to raise issues rather than to prevail on election day. Freed of the usual constraints of American politics, the consumer activist was raising real issues with a platform—labeled "The Concord Principles" because the document was unveiled in Concord, New Hampshire—that called for "the reconstruction of our democracy." At the center of the principles was a declaration: "Modern electronic communications can play a critical role in anticipating and resolving costly national problems when their owners gain regular usage, as a community intelligence, to inform, alert, and mobilize democratic citizen initiatives. Presently, these electronic broadcasting systems are overwhelmingly used for entertainment, advertising, and redundant news, certainly not a fair reflection of what a serious society needs to communicate in a complex age, locally, nationally, and globally."[3]

As Nader sketched his vision of a radically reformed media through the development of audience-run networks and the dedication of one full hour of prime-time and drive-time on all licensed stations to the purpose of informing and mobilizing the citizenry, the great college hall was charged with energy. People nudged one another, nodded in agreement, cheered, and finally awarded the consumer activist a standing ovation. "This is the first time I've come to a political event and felt a sense of hope—the first time I thought, 'Maybe we really can change things,'" Vicky Turner, a student from Bennington, said after she jostled her way to the front of the crowd and shook hands with Nader. "I'm really excited about what he's saying about television and democracy. Just imagine if we could get rid of the 30-second commercials and the sound bites and start talking about issues that matter."[4] Deborah "Arnie" Arnesen, a New Hampshire state representative who that fall would be the Democratic nominee for governor, shared Turner's enthusiasm. "Television, radio, media, that's where it's at," said Arnesen. "People know something's wrong, very wrong. Most of us don't even dare to imagine that we could change something as big as mass media. But when Nader says, 'We own the airwaves,' well, you start to think, 'Hey, we've got a right to demand something better.' You could just see the wheels turning in people's heads."[5]

Unluckily, for Turner, Arnesen and all the other people who left the Keene State College campus that night buzzing about the prospect of taking the airwaves back for the people, that year's Nader campaign was not the vehicle that was—and is—needed to shape a long-term political movement for media reform. Nader was in New Hampshire seeking write-in votes in the Democratic and Republican primaries in order to "make a little history" so that "when we talk in Washington about citizen involvement we won't be greeted by blank stares." After the New Hampshire and Massachusetts primaries, however, Nader left the trail to Bill Clinton, George Bush, and Ross Perot, and serious discussion of media as a political issue ceased for another campaign.

Yet, as the only prominent candidate for the American presidency in recent years to talk seriously about media reform, Nader proved a point that ought not be lost on citizens who want to make media the sort of political issue in this country that it is in other lands. Despite what the pundits say, when citizens begin to entertain the notion that media can be an issue—rather than something that simply happens to us, and to our democracy—they get excited. When the political imagination is freed, as Nader illustrated, the supposed apathy of the electorate can be replaced with a level of engagement that suggests the promise of American democracy might yet be made real.

So how do we free the political imagination? How do we widen the parameters of the debate to include topics that have been left off the table for generations? How do we make media an issue? To begin to find answers to these questions, let's consider how the environment has become a political issue in the United States and globally over the past 30 years. One of the leading architects of the modern green movement, former U.S. Senator Gaylord Nelson of Wisconsin, suggests that Americans would be wise to see media reform as having movement-building potential not unlike what the nascent cause of environmental protection once evidenced.

In the 1960s, Gaylord Nelson was a voice in the political wilderness, an environmentalist who was often treated by his fellow U.S. senators as a nag on issues of clean air and clean water, and who struggled to get serious media attention for what he felt was the most fundamental of all issues—the sustainability of human life on the planet. Nelson's successful effort to make the environment an issue provides a case study in both the frustrations and the opportunities that attend any struggle to broaden the public discourse. And it is notable that, today, Nelson points to mounting frustration with big media—particularly as it relates to the question of media's role in a democracy—as the sort of issue that could well energize citizens. When Nelson came to the United States Senate in 1963 as the former governor of a small progressive state, he imagined that he could quickly force environmental issues onto the national agenda. The times seemed right. Rachel Carson had published *Silent Spring*, there was a mounting awareness of and concern about pollution of America's air and water, and there were sure signs of a rising level of civic engagement that could be turned to the task of saving the earth.

But making an issue—even of something so fundamental as the environment—proved to be a far more difficult task than Nelson had expected. His hopes of convincing then-President John Kennedy, who showed an interest in the subject, to make it a focus of his administration were dashed by an assassin's bullet. And his attempts to get Kennedy's successor, Lyndon Johnson, to make the environment a priority were met with little enthusiasm. On the floor of the Senate, and in his dealings with the federal bureaucracy, Nelson encountered more than his share of closed doors. "People would say to me: We've got so many other things to deal with—Vietnam, civil rights, poverty, all these important issues—why do you keep going on about clean air, clean water, the population explosion?" Nelson recalled. "I had to explain to them that a focus on the environment didn't come at the expense of those issues. But the environment had to be an issue, there had to be space for this issue because it simply could not wait any longer. The earth was in danger, real danger. We couldn't put the issue off any longer."[6] Nelson persevered. He introduced bills, organized hearings, spoke in more than 30 states, signed up allies, kept lists, worked with nascent environmental groups and individual activists. "I had the idea of trying to get the environment on the national political agenda. It wasn't there in the 1960s," Nelson said. "Nobody campaigned on it. Hell, as recently as 1968, in the Humphrey-Nixon race, neither candidate made a single speech on the environment. They didn't think it was an important enough issue to talk to the public about. It wasn't seen as a 'vote-getter.' Can you imagine that? Today, no politician would dare say that. But at the time, that was what we were up against."[7]

Nelson's tireless activism left him with the impression that the people were far ahead of the politicians, however, and in 1969—flying home from an anti-war "teach-in" on a California campus—he hit on the notion that would in a matter of months make the environment a front-burner issue. With a handful of allies, he called for a national

"Earth Day" in April of 1970, on which he said he hoped that rallies and teach-ins would be organized to educate people about the importance of environmental issues, and about what they could do to advance them. Run out of Nelson's Senate office, with little more than a green symbol and a few enthusiastic college students to power the "movement," Earth Day mushroomed into a national phenomenon—drawing more than 20 million people to events across the country, earning blanket national and international media coverage, and turning the heads of every politician in the nation, including President Richard Nixon, who quickly signed a series of sweeping environmental protection measures. "I wouldn't have gambled on trying to create a grassroots movement if I didn't think there was support at the grassroots," says Nelson. "I had been across the country. I knew that everybody was impacted by some environmental issue. Every industrial community had an orange cloud. Every community had a polluted lake, a beach that was closed, a wetland that had disappeared. All kinds of things were going wrong. Everybody felt something was going wrong in their local area. And they noticed that the politicians were doing nothing. This was their first opportunity to demonstrate their interest and they demonstrated it in spades. The politicians looked at it and said: What the hell is this? If nothing else, politicians have to be good at sensing what the people are concerned about and they did. It worked."

Nelson proved, as have countless other American activists from John Brown to Elizabeth Cady Stanton to Mother Jones to Martin Luther King Jr., that it is possible to force an issue into the nation's political discourse—even an issue that the political and economic elites would prefer to keep off the radar. The environmental movement shared a damning feature with movements for media reform: there were no powerful monied interests that would benefit by its success. All the money was either agnostic or firmly opposed to reform. And as Saul Alinsky has pointed out, when faced with organized money, the only recourse is organized people. To determine whether the environmental movement could generate enough popular support to overcome organized money, Nelson said it had to answer three questions affirmatively. It is therefore appropriate to ask whether the media reform movement can do likewise.

The first question is: Does the issue at hand—in this case, the sorry state of media in America—affect everyone in some fundamental way? By any measure, the answer is yes.

The second question is: Is there an alternative to the status quo, a remedy, that can and should be put in place? Looking abroad we can see that the answer again is yes, though the exact contours of a U.S. reform program need to be developed.

The third question is: Do people believe they have the power to implement necessary changes and, if not, can they be made to believe anew in their ability to use democracy to set things right? Here the answer is "no," at present, and it is our job to change the answer to a "yes." We do that by building a movement on many levels and, in the course of doing so, developing a clear platform of specific media reform proposals.

To build a media reform movement will not require starting from scratch, but it will require a bold vision for structural change. There has been, for example, an "inside-the-beltway" coterie of public interest media lobbyists for decades. In the current environment of profit *über alles*, their influence is too limited, they get almost no press coverage. Therefore, they have a difficult time building popular support and are too frequently limited to outcomes that do not threaten corporate control. Yet, they do important and necessary work. In 1995, for example, the Center for Media Education organized more than 80 groups representing parents, consumers, school board members, educators, religious communities, health professionals, and children's rights advocates to call on the Federal Communications Commission to strengthen federal guidelines for children's and educational programming on commercial television stations. The groups ranged from the American Academy of Child and Adolescent Psychiatry to the Consumer Federation of America, the National Education Association, the National School Boards Association, the National Association of Elementary School Principals, the National PTA, the Institute for Mental Health Initiatives, the U.S. Catholic Conference, the United Church of Christ, and even the Indiana Extension Homemakers Association. They delivered a simple message: Government can and should regulate media in order to combat "trends that imperil our nation's health, security, and future."[8] The limits of this type of organizing became clear when the FCC's eventual mandate for "educational" children's programming permitted it to be advertising-supported, hence making for a dubious victory, if it was a victory at all. Without a movement, this is pretty much what media reform has been reduced to.

A striking example both of what grassroots organizing can contribute to media organizing, and also of the powerful barriers that are thrown up against such activism, can be found in the case of microradio broadcasting. Profound technological advances have made it possible for non-commercial community groups to use unoccupied parts of the FM radio spectrum to start up new radio stations that broadcast at 100 watts or less. Hundreds of unlicensed microbroadcasters emerged in the late 1990s, providing vitality and diverse local fare in contrast to the commercial homogeneity of the corporate radio system. After years of relentless organizing by a national movement, the FCC finally recognized the importance of microradio in early 2000 and proposed regulations to legalize it as a noncommercial activity available to community groups. Although movement activists take issue with many of the fine points of the FCC's new plan, approximately 700 new community stations will result if the FCC's proposal is fully implemented. Despite popular support, the new plan is under intense attack by commercial broadcasters—led by the National Association of Broadcasters—who oppose any new competition for listeners. At their bidding, a bill was drafted to crush the new microradio licensing plan and limit the number of new stations to a token amount: 70. At the time of this writing, the bill has passed in the House and is waiting for vote in the Senate, all with virtually no press coverage or debate.

A good deal of citizen outrage at media assumes the form of boycotts and protests that intend to shame the media giants into reforming their ways. Boycotts and protests in recent years have concerned the high levels of infantile sexual content and violence in primetime TV, demeaning portrayals of women, ethnic groups and gays and lesbians, or simply the lack of cultural diversity in entertainment programming. Likewise there has emerged, a strong movement for media literacy, which attempts to educate schoolchildren and adults about how the commercial media system operates so they may be more informed consumers. With regard to journalism, there is a "civic journalism" movement, which attempts to have journalists reform their practices to produce fare that, in theory, will provide information citizens will need to make political decisions. Most of these movements are based upon real problems, but they all shy away from structural criticism that challenges the rule of corporate and commercial interests over the media. They are therefore limited in what they can accomplish. As with the "inside-the-beltway" lobbying groups mentioned above, these efforts need to be supercharged by a popular media reform movement that puts the media giants and their commercial logic on the hot seat.

In fact, and this point can scarcely be overemphasized, the range for improvement within the existing corporate media system is extremely limited. Even those paltry public service efforts like the do-gooder TV public service announcements put together by the Ad Council are being compromised or shelved as the pressure to generate profit eliminates any time at all for noncommercial values.[9] The FCC itself has almost no room to maneuver when it attempts even the mildest infringement upon the prerogatives of the media giants. To do so invariably invites the industry's running dogs on Capitol Hill to announce that the FCC is "overstepping" its mandate and needs to back down or face getting its funding cut. Curiously, when the FCC acts aggressively to advance the corporate interest, one never hears important members of Congress bellyaching that the FCC is overstepping its bounds.[10]

There is no way around it: Structural media reform is

mandatory if we are serious about addressing the crisis of democracy in the United States. We are not alone in this conviction. During the 1990s, a grassroots media reform movement went from virtual nonexistence to becoming a notable force on the margins of the political landscape. This burgeoning media reform movement takes place on several complementary levels, all of which need to be cultivated. For example, grassroots groups have been formed in numerous communities around the nation to work on media issues. Sometimes, as in Baltimore and Chicago, these groups organize to get billboards (generally promoting alcoholic beverages) removed from working-class, usually minority residential neighborhoods. At other times they work to monitor the content of the local commercial media and to support the efforts to establish nonprofit community media and/or microradio stations. The most impressive operation may be Denver's Rocky Mountain Media Watch, which does expert analysis of local media and gives people the tools to become media activists. Likewise, local activists organize to see that cable companies fulfill their obligations for public access channels to the hilt, and many activists have been active in producing microradio services.

Local media activism is the foundation of the media reform movement, and there is much that can be done at the local level. As the Christian Coalition recognized a decade ago, an effective national political movement has as much to do with school board races as contests for presidential nominations. This is even more true when the issue is media reform, since local government has the ability to make some fundamental decisions about the media that we and our children consume.

Imagine the impact of a thousand school board candidacies in which a commitment to implement a critical media literacy curriculum was a part of the agenda. Imagine the impact of a thousand city council candidacies in which a commitment of full municipal funding for quality community access programming on cable was a feature of the platform. Imagine a thousand local media activist groups, meeting in neighborhoods and small towns, in church basements and union halls, adopting and adapting models for organizing already developed by Fairness & Accuracy in Reporting (FAIR).[11] Imagine ten thousand letter writers penning regular challenges to local media that fail to cover the broad diversity of issues in their communities. And imagine if these local letter writers were linked—through the Internet, phone trees, and direct mail—so that they could marshal their energy to exercise grassroots pressure on the broadcast networks and the Congress. This is the sort of daily, "in-your-life" activism that many Americans are already involved in, and that many, many more are ready to embrace.

In the past year, we have recognized a marked increase in local media activism, particularly around issues of maintaining daily newspaper competition. In Hawaii, in the fall of 1999, Rupert Phillips, the owner of the *Honolulu Star-Bulletin,* announced that he would shut the well-regarded newspaper in return for a $26.5 million payoff from the Gannett newspaper chain, the owner of the state's other major daily newspaper, the *Honolulu Advertiser*. Phillips admitted that the *Star-Bulletin* was making money, and that the newspaper was on a roll after a number of major investigative reporting coups. But, he said, the 12 percent profit he was a pulling out of Hawaii "wasn't enough," so he decided to take the money and allow Gannett to create a monopoly.

Similar payoffs have created newspaper monopolies in other cities, such as Miami and Nashville, and they have resulted in a narrowing of the discourse as they have killed feisty smaller papers that tended to be more ideological and more aggressive in their reporting. Recognizing the threat, a broad coalition of Hawaiians organized to prevent the closing of their state's second-largest newspaper. The "Save Our *Star-Bulletin*" (SOS) movement pulled together the state's strongest unions, including the proudly radical International Longshore and Warehouse Union, the Newspaper Guild, community activists, and political leaders. They got the state's Congressional delegation to demand that the U.S. Justice Department investigate the closure deal as a violation of federal antitrust laws and the Newspaper Preservation Act—which had allowed Gannett and Phillips to develop a highly profitable Joint Operating Agreement relationship in return for the commitment to maintain two competing newspaper voices. Governor Ben Cayetano endorsed the SOS movement and Hawaii Attorney General Earl Anzai filed an anti-trust lawsuit against the shutdown, which was stalled in October when Federal Judge Alan Kay granted an injunction preventing Phillips from shuttering the *Star-Bulletin*. As a result of the unprecedented citizen activism, Honolulu remains a two-newspaper town, pending a trial to determine if Gannett's payoff to Phillips violated anti-trust laws. "We drew a line in the sand in Hawaii because we feel this is a winnable fight," explained Ray Camacho, an ILWU official in Hawaii. "There's a certain corporate arrogance because they've done it [shut down competing newspapers] elsewhere and weren't stopped. But we're isolated here in the Pacific so it's almost like a laboratory setting where you can see the impacts of closing down one paper where there are no others in outlying areas to pick up the slack like on the mainland."[12]

As it turns out, this burgeoning anti-monopoly movement is not isolated on the islands of the Pacific. In November 1999, San Francisco Supervisor Tom Ammiano, who stunned local pols by building a grassroots progressive mayoral campaign, asked the city attorney to file an antitrust lawsuit to block the sale of the locally-owned *San Francisco Chronicle* newspaper to its competitor, the Hearst Corp.–owned *San Francisco Examiner*. Ammiano and San Francisco media activists were inspired to make their move by the success of Hawaii's SOS campaign, and by evidence of a renewed interest on the part of the Justice Department in antitrust prosecutions.[13]

The willingness of political, union, and community leaders in San Francisco and Honolulu to ask tough questions about media mergers and monopolies has had an impact that suggests the potential for media activism is far greater even than its most optimistic proponents might suggest. Months after both the *Honolulu Star-Bulletin* and the *San Francisco Examiner* were supposed to be buried in the newspaper graveyard, they are still on the streets. Indeed, the bible of print journalism, *Editor and Publisher* magazine, ran a January feature story hailing the revitalization of the *Star-Bulletin*. The headline boomed: "Catching a brand-new wave: *Honolulu Star-Bulletin* rides the curl into 2000 after nearly wiping out in 1999."

The targeted efforts in Honolulu and San Francisco

to make media giants obey federal law represent one side of the new media activist movement. Of equal or greater significance are ongoing efforts by activists around the country to make media an issue everyday, and to create their own media.

The impressive work of independent media activists in Seattle during last November's protests against the policies of the World Bank, and during April's Mobilization for Global Justice in Washington, offers a powerful model not just for challenging corporate media but for changing it. Independent Media Centers were formed by movement-oriented print, audio, video, and photo journalists, who distributed minute-by-minute coverage to the world by way of their web site, www.indymedia.org, and who bought satellite time to pipe down daily video coverage to hundreds of community access television stations nationwide. Tapes of the video coverage also found their way onto mainstream evening news reports. Why? Because low-budget, grassroots "Indy Media" reporters were often where the action was, while their corporate competitors were playing catch up. As new technologies make it easier for media activists to tell stories in their communities, the role and the impact of independent media will expand—not just during mass mobilizations, but everyday.

In many communities across the country, that's already happening.

In Iowa City, Iowa, for example, Karen Kubby is just stepping down after ten years of service as an independent progressive member of the City Council. Kubby has always recognized the importance of media activism in all its forms. She has made "in-your-face" demands of local media, and she has adopted the "do-it-yourself" model—even creating "The Kubby Campaign Corner," a weekly cable access program on which she has explained how genuine progressive taxation would work, told people how they can fight cutbacks in library hours, described the damage to local development that comes when money is poured into defense spending at the federal level, and even discussed the media. "We've used the Council position and the cable access programs to make people aware that media has a role to play in a democracy, that it's a vehicle we can and should be able to use to get ideas out, to get discussions going, to get things happening in a community, at the state level and, someday I hope, nationally," says Kubby, who is active in the Socialist Party of Norman Thomas and Eugene Victor Debs. "I always tell people: You can't separate a desire for more democracy from a willingness to get involved in media work. And, for most of us, the place we get involved is in our hometowns, in our neighborhoods."[14]

Since most of the key policy shifts necessarily must be implemented at the federal level, the development of a movement for media reform requires regional and national organization. Here, too, there have been impressive developments in recent years. The aforementioned FAIR was launched in the late 1980s and has developed an impressive national operation, with 10 full-time staffers producing important research reports on the operations of the corporate media system. These reports are circulated nationally though FAIR's excellent publication *Extra!*. FAIR's work provides a measure of the intellectual oxygen needed for the growth of a strong and sustained media reform movement. Complementing

FAIR are two new national media reform groups, both of which were formed in 1999 and both of which are now working to establish local chapters. People for Better Television crusades for the strengthening of regulations that require broadcasters to perform at least minimal public service in return for free use of citizen-owned airwaves. Citizens for Independent Public Broadcasting works to decommercialize and democratize public radio and television. The necessary next step will be the formation of a coalition group to bring local and national groups together, so they will not compete with each other and so they may strategize and maximize the use of scarce resources. Such a media reform coalition group would also have to establish working relationships with similar movements in other nations in order to coordinate global campaigns targeted to influence the United Nations, the International Labor Organization, the World Trade Organization, and other powerful grouping that have influence over multinational corporations, or that serve as forums for discussions of media ownership and quality.

As impressive as the work of existing media reform groups at the local, regional, and national levels may be, however, they will not be sufficient to win the battle. Absent for far too long and to far too great an extent from media reform activism have been the cause's natural allies, organizations that should be sympathetic to media reform and that have been active in other nations. We refer, for example, to groups representing organized labor, teachers, librarians, civil libertarians, artists, religious affiliations, and civil rights. There has been some movement in this regard. For example, the National Organization for Women, many disability rights groups, as well as a number of gay and lesbian organizations, have developed effective and influential critiques of mainstream media coverage of issues concerning their communities—and, increasingly, of the media structures that maintain stereotypes. Both the NAACP and the Rainbow/PUSH Action Network have targeted media as a central focus for their activities—organizing forums, sending leaders to testify before Congress and raising tough questions about federal policies regarding minority ownership of broadcast outlets. The United Church of Christ has been doing good work for years. Likewise, media workers' unions have been warming up to media reform as their members have seen the disastrous implications for their work that result from concentrated corporate control and hypercommercialism. Other professional groups are entering the fray. The American Academy of Pediatrics went so far as to formally resolve in 1999 that commercial television was a public health hazard for children.[15] But these efforts need to be expanded exponentially and these groups have to be brought together to strategize and maximize their effect. Solo ventures, however well organized and well intended, cannot begin to address the issues raised by media conglomeration and commercialization.

Considering the scope of the issues at stake, some might even suggest that a united front would be insufficient to take on the media conglomerates, their lobbyists and the politicians they have bought. But we believe such a united front could accomplish a great deal.

Even in these days of right-wing Congressional hegemony, it is important to be mindful of the fact that progressive religious denominations, consumer groups, student organizations, civil rights and women's rights organizations, critics of the drug war and the prison-industrial complex, the labor movement, and farm groups provide a powerful grassroots base from which to pressure for change. If there is a single lesson that came out of "the Battle in Seattle," where progressive forces coalesced to take on the forces of corporate capital embodied by the World Trade Organization, it is that the old slogan, "the people united will never be defeated" has more validity even than many on the left have believed.

It is clear that an energized core of progressive reformers—linked through the Internet, phone trees, and direct mail—can have a powerful influence during debates over media regulation issues that regularly come before the FCC or Congress. Had some coherent organization been in place just five years ago, it might well have derailed the atrocious 1996 Telecommunications Act—just as energized coalitions of labor, farm, and environmental groups halted "fast-track" trade expansion and the Multilateral Agreement on Investment. The Telecommunications Act slid through Congress largely because the groups that have been effected by that law were for the most part unaware of the Congressional deliberations in the months and years leading up to its passage.

In a similar fashion, media reformers need to work hand-in-hand with closely related campaigns to challenge corporate influence, particularly efforts to make schools advertising and commercial-free zones and movements to address the political campaign spending crisis that is destroying the integrity of electoral democracy in the United States. Both of these issues are first cousins to media reform. The commercialization of schools is being pushed by the same forces that benefit from the corporate media system, while the corporate media—primary recipients of campaign spending in the form of TV political ads—are the leading lobby that opposes any and all campaign finance reform.

In reaching out to new groups and, ultimately, to the general public, media reformers will discover something exhilarating: This is an issue that cuts across the political spectrum. So-called conservatives share progressives' dismay at the morally bankrupt commercial carpet-bombing of children and, indeed, all of us. So-called conservatives do not like trash journalism and despise TV political ads. Polling has suggested that there is virtually no difference in the attitudes of progressives and conservatives regarding these issues. Many business people are appalled at the corruption and unfairness of a system that lets corporate media giants get favorable regulations and subsidies behind closed doors in Washington. It is striking that the legion of conservative media critics—you know, the ones that have been complaining about the "liberal" media for the past 30 years—have pretty much backed away from that theme in recent years. The right wing dominance of the talking head jobs in our media along with the corporate commercial clobbering of journalism have made that argument nonsensical, except to the Limbaughs and Ollie Norths of the world, who incongruously equate Wall Street's favorite son Bill Clinton with Eugene Debs and Che Guevara. Instead the right-wing media critics now play a tune similar to that of childrens' rights activists, emphasizing the asinine excesses of commercially driven culture.[16] But conservative critics, in the end, are handcuffed by their allegiance to the maintenance of corporate and commercial rule, so they are incapable of providing real explanations for, and real solutions to, the problems they describe.

So it will be a progressive media reform movement that realizes the endless potential of an issue that can engage and energize broad—even unlikely—coalitions.

Ultimately, however, viable media reform cannot succeed as a "single issue" cause, no matter how many organizations coalesce to support it. The issue is too abstract, our society is too depoliticized, and the forces arrayed against it are too powerful. What is necessary, in the end, is for media reform to be advanced as part of a progressive platform for democratic reform across society. The foundation of a broader progressive platform will be the demand for social justice and an attack upon social inequality and the moral stench of a society operated purely along commercial lines. In the United States today, the richest one percent of the population has as much money to spend as the poorest 100 million Americans, double the ratio for just 20 years earlier.[17] The political system reinforces this inequality by being, as is now roundly acknowledged, a plaything for big business where the interests of the balance of society have been pushed to the margins if not forgotten.[18] The corporate media system reinforces this inequality and rule of the market and limits the possibility of democratic reform. In sum, media reform is inexorably intertwined with broader democratic reform; they rise and fall together.

Hence we return to the point that emerged forcefully in the analysis of media reform around the world: the importance of political parties to provide necessary leadership and to force the issue into the political arena. In the United States, both the Republican and Democratic

Parties, with only a few prominent exceptions, have been and are in the pay of the corporate media and communication giants. It is unlikely that any breakthroughs can be expected there until much spadework is done. The logical place to begin that spadework ought to be the small parties and factions of the left in America, the New Party, the Greens, the Labor Party, Democratic Socialists of America, Americans for Democratic Action, and U.S. Action. In our view, all of these groups need to incorporate media reform issues into their platforms and their visions. Ideally, these organizations, which have remarkably similar stances on a host of issues, might adopt a shared vision—perhaps as a step toward building the sort of labor, left, green, feminist, people of color coalitions seen in New Zealand's Alliance Party, Iceland's Alliance, and other Third Left groupings. In Wisconsin, already, the Greens and New Party activists are working together on joint projects. In Washington, D.C., the Greens have merged with the D.C. Statehood Party.

Sadly, however, these new left parties have dropped the ball concerning media so far, with only one or two exceptions. As U.S. Rep. Bernie Sanders, the Vermont independent who is the only socialist member of the U.S. House of Representatives, and who has made media reform a central issue for over a decade has noted: "This is an issue that is absolutely vital to democracy, and that only the left can address. The New Party, the Green Party, the Labor Party, progressive Democrats should be all over this issue. But, for most of the left, it's not even on the agenda."[19] This has to change, and change soon, both for the sake of media reform and for the sake of these parties and progressive politics in the United States. It is difficult for us to imagine a better place to build trust and cooperation across these left groupings than with a shared response to media, which has been so devastatingly dismissive of third-party initiatives, save those of billionaire hot dogs Ross Perot and Donald Trump.

Who would contribute to the shaping of a progressive media reform platform. Ideally, it would be shaped as similar platforms in Sweden, Finland, Canada, and other lands have been. Local and national groups working on media reform would participate. There would also be significant input from media unions, such as the Newspaper Guild, the National Writers Union, and the American Federation of Television and Radio Artists. We believe these groups could get the ball rolling by coming together in support of a set of basic principles not unlike those advanced by Britain's Campaign for Press and Broadcast Freedom.[20]

There is every reason to believe that these groups could ultimately agree on an agenda that calls for basic reforms, such as:

➤Expansion of funding for traditional public-service broadcasting with an eye toward making it fully non-commercial and democratically accountable. In particular, substantial new funding should be provided for the development of news and public affairs programming that will fill the gap created by the collapse of serious newsgathering by the networks and their local affiliates.

➤Development of non-commercial, community-run, public-access television and radio systems that are distinct from public-service broadcasting and that are deeply rooted in local communities. As part of this initiative, the federal government should remove barriers to the development of microradio initiatives. Seed money, similar to that provided by government and foundations for economic development in low-income and minority communities, should be targeted toward groups seeking to develop microradio.

➤Setting far stricter standards for commercial broadcasters in exchange for granting them broadcast licenses. For example, why not ban or strictly limit advertising on childrens' programs and on news broadcasts? Why not take a percentage of the broadcasters' revenues and set it aside for creative people and journalists to control time set aside for children's shows and newscasts? Why not make a condition of receiving a broadcast license that the broadcaster will not carry any paid political advertising during electoral campaigns? And that they will provide free time to all, liberally defined, viable candidates?

➤Creation of a broad initiative to limit advertising in general, using regulation and taxation to prevent commercial saturation.

➤Reassertion of anti-trust protections in order to limit the amount of media that can be owned by one firm. Why not, for example, limit radio stations to one per owner? The benefits of concentrated ownership accrue entirely to owners, not to the public. Make it government policy to encourage diversity of ownership and diversity of editorial opinions, as was intended by the First Amendment. There should, as well, be a reassertion of traditional restrictions on cross-ownership of media within particular communities

➤Renewing the commitment of the United States government to develop incentives aimed at encouraging and protecting minority ownership of broadcast and cable outlets.

➤Promotion of newspaper and magazine competition through the use of tax deductions or subsidies. One approach might allow taxpayers to deduct the cost of a limited number of newspaper and magazine subscriptions—as some professionals and academics now do. Such an initiative would boost the circulations of publications from across the ideological spectrum, but would be particularly helpful to publications that target low-income, working-class, and elderly citizens, as well as students. Significantly lowered postal fees for nonprofit publications that have minimal advertising might also be appropriate.

➤Strengthen the position of media unions by encouraging the development of a stronger role for workers in determining the editorial content of news publications and broadcast news. As in European countries, union protections in the U.S. should be strengthened in order to assure that working journalists are free to perform their duties with an eye toward serving the public interest.

➤Develop a new national program of subsidies for film and cultural production, particularly by members of ethnic and racial minority groups, women, low-income citizens, and others who frequently have a hard time finding market support for their artistic expressions.

➤Use tax breaks and subsidies to promote creation of publishing and production cooperatives and other arts and culture vehicles designed to provide non-commercial outlets for writers and artists to bring meaningful, controversial, and substantive work to mass audiences. One proposal put forth by economist Dean Baker would let any American redirect $150 from their tax payments to any nonprofit medium of their choice. This could funnel as much as $25 billion into nonprofit media and create a very healthy competition among new and revitalized outlets for democratic and cultural expression. All this could be done without any government official gumming up the works.

In combination, these proposals would go a long way toward creating a strong democratic sector on the rapidly commercializing Internet, as every medium today has a web component almost by definition. By the same token, media reformers must demand that there be formal hearings and public deliberations on the future of digital communication systems. At present the crucial technical decisions are being made quietly behind closed doors to the benefit of the corporate community. That has to be stopped.

Consider, for just a moment, if you will, what the U.S. media landscape would look like if all of these reforms were enacted. There would be no government censorship of media content. Any private individual could launch a commercial newspaper, or magazine, or website, and operate with all the freedom they currently enjoy—and with all the protection intended by the framers of the First Amendment. But Wall Street and Madison Avenue would no longer dominate our culture and journalism. There would be a variety of well-funded alternatives, both local and national, across all media. In this new world the marketplace of ideas would be a vibrant flowering garden, not the strip mall of chain stores we currently experience. Such media reform would not guarantee the end of injustice, poverty, or human misery, but it would provide a far superior basis for our society to address and confront the important issues of our times.

Is this a utopian vision? Only in the sense that women's suffrage, civil rights, and Social Security were utopian ideals at the beginning of the 20th century.

We understand that these reforms will not be enacted in isolation from other social change, nor will they happen overnight. We emphasize the need for building a specific political platform because a touchstone is needed. The single mom in Providence, the factory worker in Pittsburgh, the farmer outside of Des Moines, and the out-of-work actor in Los Angeles, all of whom recognize that media needs to change, deserve something better than a cacophony of suggestions. There needs to be a coherent base agenda to which activists can commit, in the full knowledge that they are free to—indeed, encouraged to—add local, regional, and national variations on the theme. As well, there ought to be something that people can point to when they are asked by others: "What is it that you want?" Once activists have a basic platform around which to organize, they can take it to their unions, their cooperatives, their churches, their community organizations, and ask that it become a part of the agenda of those institutions.

Will there be challenges in getting the parties of the left—the Greens, New Party, and Labor Party—to join Democratic Socialists of America, Americans for Democratic Action, U.S. Action, and a host of other pressure groups in signing on to a common media-reform agenda? Of course. But we believe that an awareness of the dire current circumstance and a hunger for change will prove to be a powerful coalition-building force. "I think there are a lot of people in these groups who talk about media all the time, complain about media all the time, but haven't known what to do. If there was a document, a platform, they could focus on, yes, sure, I think you'd see a lot of support for it," says author Barbara Ehrenreich, a longtime co-chair of DSA.[21]

Just as media reform should be a part of the agenda of the parties of the left, so it also must have a place in whatever battles may be waged to alter the direction of the Democratic party. The party is in flux today. Pulled adrift from its populist and New Deal moorings, it has been remade at the national level by the Democratic Leadership Council, a neoliberal grouping that has sought to create a Democratic party that is "good for business" or, as the Reverend Jesse Jackson puts it, "Democrats for the Leisure Class." At the grassroots, however, the Democratic party remains a more progressive entity. Some progressive Democrats are already willing to push the topic of media reform ahead in their party and on Capitol Hill. U.S. Senator Paul Wellstone (D-MN), one of the few members of Congress who regularly addresses media issues, puts it well when he says, "There's no question that we have to start talking in a serious way about media, about media mergers and monopolies, about the balance between public and commercial television, about how we can encourage more diversity in ownership and in content. There's no question that we ought to be talking about the role that media plays in a democracy where most people don't vote. There's no question of any of this."[22]

Would a platform fight on media issues force the Democratic party to confront its drift to the right, as well as the disconnection between its DLC-dominated leadership and its more progressive mass membership? Possibly. But, at the least, it would identify media as an issue—an issue on which it is not merely reasonable, but also necessary, to do battle. Struggles of this sort would, as well, draw sympathetic members of Congress into the fray. In addition to Wellstone and Sanders, a growing number of Congressional Black Caucus, Hispanic Caucus, and Progressive Caucus members have expressed an interest. Indeed, one of the most powerful figures in the House, U.S. Rep. John Conyers (D-MI), the ranking Democrat on the House Judiciary Committee, has attended sessions on media monopoly and diversity organized by the Rainbow-PUSH Coalition. "I think it would be very interesting, very important, to hold hearings on some of these issues," says Conyers, who would chair the Judiciary Committee in a Democrat-controlled House.[23]

Platform debates and Congressional hearings, while important, cannot be the purpose of this initiative, however. They are merely tools for promoting the notion that media can be an issue in America. It is the implanting of that notion that we believe will lead to a leap of faith on the part of millions of Americans, who will recognize that mounting a challenge to media monoliths and their political patrons is no more an uphill climb than was mounting a challenge to the corporate polluters of the 1960s and the 1970s, or the WTO of the 1990s. That realization, the essential third component of Gaylord Nelson's equation, is critical to unleashing the sort of broad grassroots action that will finally make media a genuine and ongoing issue in America. "We go around with all this frustration over media. But most of us think it's just something that happens to us," explains Patty Allen, a labor activist who worked 23 years on an Oscar Mayer meatpacking line in Wisconsin and got turned on to media issues by Ralph Nader. "When I first heard Nader say that we own the airwaves and that we have a right to demand something better in return, I remember how liberating it felt. I was saying, 'Wow, now that I know this, what do I do? Where do I sign up? How can I demand a change?' I think there's a lot of people like me all over this country who are ready. But we need a sense that we're not just wasting our time."[24]

The exciting shift that will come if and when media really does become an issue in America will not be measured in the passage of a particular bill in Congress—though we are convinced that, if media becomes an issue, important reform legislation will eventually be enacted. Rather, it will be best measured in the awakening of working people like Patty Allen, who have for decades been neglected, dismissed, and beaten down[25] by a media that tells them there is no alternative to a steady diet of O. J. Simpson, Monica Lewinsky, exercise tips, and weather pages. When media is an issue, people like Patty Allen will be demanding more from the media conglomerates that dominate our discourse and from the government that is supposed to regulate them. People like Patty will also demand more of themselves. They will start to see media not as something that happens to them, but rather as something that they have a right and an ability to shape—at the national level and at the local level.

Where does this lead?

We believe that a media reform movement with clear goals and a clear strategy for achieving them will be a fundamental building block of a broad crusade for democratic renewal in America—a bold, powerful and ultimately successful initiative that has the potential to make this nation's promise for democracy real. It will be a movement that takes an issue too long neglected and pushes that concern to the center of the national debate. It will be a movement that gives us an answer to the powers-that-be who seek constantly to divert us from issues of consequence. It will be a movement that empowers us to respond to their distractions and deceits by laughing in their faces and saying: "It's the media, stupid."

NOTES

CHAPTER ONE

1: Some of the points made in this section are elaborated upon in detail in Robert W. McChesney, *Rich Media, Poor Democracy: Communication Politics in Dubious Times* (New York: The New Press, 2000).

2: Lee Hall, "Gates Top Dog of Forbes Fat Cats," *Electronic Media*, June 28, 1999, p. 8.

3: Christopher Stern, "Radio Receives Rivals by Satellite," *Variety*, June 28-July 11, 1999, p. 5. See also, Susan J. Douglas, *Listening In: Radio and the American Imagination* (New York: Times Books, 1999).

4: Stuart Elliott, "Advertising," *The New York Times*," July 1, 1999, p. C6.

5: Ira Teinowitz, "Study: Net Prime-Time Clutter Worsens," *Advertising Age*, April 12, 1999, p. 36.

6: Wayne Friedman, "GM Goes Looney for Warner Bros. in $200 Mil Deal," *Advertising Age*, August 2, 1999, pp. 1, 48.

7: Chuck Ross, "Warner Bros. to Test 'Virtual' Ad Concept," *Advertising Age*, May 17, 1999, pp. 1, 64.

8: "Plug and Play," *The Economist*, July 24, 1999, p. 61.

9: Scott Donaton, "CBS, TV's New Bauble Seller, Bloats When it Should Blush," *Advertising Age*, June 28, 1999, p. 32; Chuck Ross, "NBC's 'Passions' to join TV merchandising parade," *Advertising Age*, June 28, 1999, p. 64.

10: Sally Beatty, "Hilfiger Snubs Madison Avenue, Hires Cable Network to Create Ads," *The New York Times*, August 10, 1999, p. B7.

11: Andrew Edgecliffe-Johnson, "Girl Power, Spending Power," *Financial Times*, August 26, 1999, p. 16.

12: Alex Kuczynski, "The Truman Show," *The New York Times Magazine*, August 1, 1999, p. 35.

13: Alex Kuczynski, "At Magazines, the Art of Stirring Debate Seems Lost," *The New York Times*, August 9, 1999, p. C11.

14: Dennis Harvey, "Detroit Rock City," *Variety*, August 9-15, 1999, p. 39.

15: Peter Bart comments, *Brill's Content*, December 1999/January 2000, p. 97.

16: Christian Moerk and Claude Brodesser, "In H'W'D, the Show Must Go On," *Variety*, September 27-October 3, 1999, p. 29.

17: Richard Katz, "Fresh Shocks Boost Cable Dox," *Variety*, April 5-11, 1999, pp. 47, 60; Bill Carter and Lawrie Mifflin, "Mainstream TV Bets on 'Gross-Out' Humor," *The New York Times*, July 19, 1999, pp. C1, C10;

Alan Frutkin, "Is Sex Getting Hotter?" *Mediaweek*, July 19, 1999, p. 10; John Dempsey, "Summer Sizzle," *Variety*, August 2-8, 1999, pp. 23, 27.

18: Richard Morris, "What's Dumbing Down Journalism?" *The Washington Post National Weekly Edition*, April 5, 1999, p. 34.

19: David Halberstam, "Preface," in Bill Kovach and Tom Rosenstiel, *Warp Speed: America in the Age of Mixed Media* (New York: The Century Foundation Press, 1999), p. ix.

20: Larry Sabato, *Feeding Frenzy: How Attack Journalism Has Transformed American Politics* (New York: The Free Press, 1991), p. 227.

21: Josef Adalian, "TV News Take Station Break," *Variety*, April 12-18, 1999, pp. 1, 79.

22: Sally Beatty, "CNN to Expand Business News 2 1/2 Hours Daily," *The Wall Street Journal*, July 19, 1999, p. B5.

23: Jon Lafayette, "Wanna Puff Piece? WDSI Tried to Oblige," *Electronic Media*, July 19, 1999, pp. 3, 34.

24: David Zurawik, "How a Newspaper's Deal Soured," *The Baltimore Sun*, Nov. 11, 1999.

25: See special issue of *Extra!*, July-August 1999 for thorough treatment of mainstream press coverage of the Kosovo war.

26: Alexis de Tocqueville, *Democracy in America, Vol. II* (New York: Vintage, 1945) p. 119.

27: Susan Kuchinskas, "Lights, Camera, Online!" *Mediaweek*, June 21, 1999, pp. 66-70.

28: John Markoff, "Not a Great Equalizer After All?" *The New York Times*, June 21, 1999, p. C4.

29: Diane Mermigas, "Throwing Money at the Net," *Electronic Media*, November 1, 1999, p. 16; Richard Siklos, Linda Himelstein, Ronald Grover, and Catherine Yang, "Dot.com or Bust," *Business Week*, September 13, 1999, pp. 78-82.

30: Russell Shaw, "Get the Goods on CNN.com," *Electronic Media*, May 10, 1999, p. 14; Wendy Bounds, "Magazines Face Ethics Questions As They Push Online Ventures," *The Wall Street Journal*, June 21, 1999, pp. B1, B4.; Mike France, "Journalism's Online Credibility Gap," *Business Week*, October 11, 1999, pp. 122-124.

31: Deborah McGregor, "Digital Divide Grows as Internet Use Soars," *Financial Times*, July 9, 1999, p. 7.

32: See, for example, Jeffrey H. Birnbaum, "Follow the Money," *Fortune*, December 6, 1999, pp. 207-208; Kim McAvey, "Industry Lobbyists Have 'Real Clout'," *Broadcasting & Cable*, September 6, 1999, p. 10.

33: David E. Rosenbaum, "TV Ads by Congressional Wives Are a Sweet Deal for All Involved," *The New York Times*, July 13, 1999, pp. A1, A15.

34: Schroeder interview, October 11, 1999.

35: Poll for Center for Media Education, conducted by Mark Cooper,

Ph.D., of Citizens Research. The questions were asked of 514 men and 513 women in a random-digit dial national sample August 24-27, 1995.

36: Poll for People for Better TV, conducted by Lake Snell Perry & Associates, May, 1999).

37: Pew Research Center national telephone poll of 1,203 adults, conducted Feb. 18-21, 1999.

38: ibid.

CHAPTER TWO

1: Jim Anderton, campaign speeches and statements, Sept. 26, 1999.

2: "Broadcasting" and "Arts and Culture" policy statements, *The Alliance*, Sept./Oct. 1999.

3: ibid.

4: "Variety's Global 50," *Variety*, August 23-29, 1999, p. A49.

5: Diane Mermigas, "More Media Firms Join Global Roster," *Electronic Media*, April 12, 1999, p. 47.

6: Elizabeth Guider, "House of Mouse Expands," *Variety*, June 28-July 11, 1999, p. 27.

7: Allen Eyles, "Worldwide Clout," *Variety*, June 21-27, 1999, p. 48.

8: "Variety International Box Office," *Variety*, August 2-8, 1999, p. 14.

9: Frank Rose, "Think Globally, Script Locally," *Fortune*, November 8, 1999, pp. 156-160; Elizabeth Guider, "Sony Ups Its Local Payoff," *Variety*, July 26-August 6, 1999, p. 23; "The Weakling Kicks Back," *The Economist*, July 3, 1999, p. 56; Andrew Paxman, "Sony Makes Dinero from Latino," *Variety*, April 12-18, 1999. p. 31.

10: "Rupert Goes to Bollywood," *The Economist*, October 2, 1999, pp. 68, 73; Amy Barrett, "News Corp. Finally Gains a Foothold in Europe," *The Wall Street Journal*, July 27, 1999, pp. B1, B4.

11: "Hollywood Gives 'Bollywood' Another Try with Movie Forays," *Variety Deal Memo*, November 22, 1999, pp. 1, 2.

12: Steve Donahue, "Liberty Media Buys Stake in GlobalCom," *Electronic Media*, September 13, 1999, p. 3; Gordon Cramb and Louise Kehoe, "Microsoft to Invest in European Cable TV," *Financial Times*, September 8, 1999, p. 16.

13: Mark Mulligan and Ken Warn, "Return of the Conquistador," *Financial Times*, June 29, 1999, p. 13.

14: Andrew Ross Sorkin, "Merger in Britain Creates Largest Publisher," *The New York Times*, July 31, 1999, p. B2; Stanley Reed, "The Yank Who's King of British Cable," *Business Week*, August 9, 1999, pp. 46-47; Felicity Barringer, "Gannett Offers $1.5 Billion In British Deal," *The New York Times*, June 25, 1999, pp. C1, C8.

15: David Owen, "Vivendi Chief Urges Europe to Think Big," *Financial Times*, May 10, 1999, p. 23.

16: John Tagliabue, "A Media World to Conquer," *The New York Times*, July 7, 1999, pp. C1, C5.

17: Paul Betts, "Fininvest to Focus on European Media Sector," *Financial Times*, April 21, 1999, p. 21; Michael Williams, "Global Ambition," *Variety*, June 28-July 11, 1999, pp. 32, 64; Marlene Edmunds, "SBS Tightens Euro Hold," *Variety*, June 14-20, 1999, p. 23.

18: Kathryn Kranhold and Steven Lipin, "Leo, McManus Merge to Form New Ad Giant," *The Wall Street Journal*, November 3, 1999, pp. B1, B4; Stuart Elliott, "Madison Avenue Sees Another Spate of Deals, Including Some Acquisitions Overseas," *The New York Times*, July 27, 1999, p, C2; Joy Dietrich, "Global Ad Decisions Centralized," *Advertising Age*, June 14, 1999, p. 70.

19: Andy Stern, "EC Panel Issues Warning to BBC on Fees," *Variety*, October 18-24, 1999, p. 32.

20: "The BBC's Begging Bowl," *The Economist*, August 7, 1999, p. 17.

21: Jim Anderton, "Sack the Radio NZ Board for Incompetence," party statement, June 16, 1999.

22: Vicki Bourne, parliamentary debate transcript, Australian Parliamentary Library, March 31, 1999.

23: Metin Munir, "Barons and Editors Hold Key to Power," *Financial Times*, June 15, 1999, p. 14; Leyla Boulton, "Media Takes Back Seat in Turkey," *Financial Times*, September 6, 1999, p. 17.

24: Andrea Mandel-Campbell, "Mexican Mayor Urged to Quit after Slaying," *Financial Times*, June 9, 1999, p. 6; Leslie Moore, "Uproar over Slain TV Comedian," *Electronic Media*, June 14, 1999, p. 55; Sally Bowen, "TV Tamed as Peru's Election Approaches," *Financial Times*, August 24, 1999, p. 5.

25: Fahran Bokhari, May 10, 1999, p. 3; Mark Landler, "A Free-Spoken Editor Won't Be Back," *The New York Times*, July 31, 1999, p. A4; "The Meaning of Freedom," *The Economist*, July 31, 1999, p. 38.

26: John F. Burns, "Arab TV Gets a New Slant: Newscasts Without Censorship," *The New York Times*, July 4, 1999, pp. A1, A6.

27: Robert Fisk, quoted in "21st Century Media," *The Campaign for Press and Broadcast Freedom*, June, 1996.

28: For an exception, see "FT Journalist Killed by East Timor Gunmen," *Financial Times*, September 23, 1999, p. 1.

29: See McChesney, *Rich Media, Poor Democracy*, ch. 2.

30: See Erla Zwingle, "A World Together," *National Geographic*, August 1999, pp. 6-33.

31: Manjeet Kripalani, "Capitalist Generation," *Business Week*, October 11, 1999, pp. 128E2-128E8.

32: Roger Thurow, "For Many Czechs, 'Velvet' Revolution Has a Course Edge," *The Wall Street Journal*, November 30, 1999, pp. A1, A8.

33: http://www.architects.com/cpbf/cpbf.htm

34: Pamela Mendels, "Plan Calls for Self-Policing of the Internet," *The New York Times*, September 20, 1999, p. C4; Diane Mermigas, "Global Group Self-policing Net," *Electronic Media*, September 20, 1999, p. 31.

35: Andrew Balls, "Information Revolution 'Risks Further Dividing Rich and Poor'," *Financial Times*, July 12, 1999, p. 4.

36: Judith Miller, "Globalization Widens Rich-Poor Gap, U.N. Report Says," *The New York Times*, July 13, 1999, p. A8.

37: Elizabeth Olson, "Free Markets Leave Women Worse Off, Unicef Says," *The New York Times*, September 23, 1999, p. A5.

38: "GM Bosses Want to Pull Out of U.K.," *The Independent*, Sept. 5, 1999.

39: Tony Benn, interview, June, 23, 1999.

40: Huw Richards, *The Bloody Circus: The Daily Herald and the Left*, (Pluto Press, 1997), p. 2.

41: ibid, p. 27.

42: Interview with Tony Benn, Oct. 7, 1999.

43: Labour Party, Policy Guide, Feb. 1992, p 30.

44: Richards, p. 13.

45: Dan Glaister and Andrew Culf, "National Heritage" section, *The Election: A Voters Guide*, (Fourth Estate, 1997, p. 132-133.

46: Francis Elliott, "Murdoch Linked to Secret TV Talks During Jiang Visit," *Scotland on Sunday*, October 24, 1999, p. 1.

47: Benn, June 23, 1999.

48: Gregor Gysi, *A Necessary Response to Gerhard Schroeder and Tony Blair*, Rosa Luxemburg Foundation, August, 1999.

49: Interview with Svend Robinson, September 20, 1997.

50: ibid.

51: John Nichols, "The English Lesson," *The Progressive*, June, 1997.

52: "Former Communists Surge In Berlin Municipal Voting," *The New York Times*, Oct. 11, 1999.

53: Program of the Left Alliance Party, adopted May 1995.

54: "For a World in Solidarity," adopted by the 1993 Left Party Congress, Sweden, p. 1.

55: "Program of the Left Alliance Party," adopted May, 1998.

56: ibid.

57: ibid, p. 3.

58: ibid, p. 18.

59: ibid, p. 18.

60: Interviews with Left party activists, Sept. 1997.

61: Jeremy Slater, "EU Lets Stand Toy Ad Ban," *Advertising Age International*, August 1999, pp. 1, 11.

62: Robinson interview.

63: Interviews with Workers Party activists, Sept., 1997.

64: COSATU Parliamentary Submission on the Broadcasting Bill, Sept. 11, 1998.

65: "21st Century Media: Media Manifesto of the Campaign for Press and Broadcast Freedom," June, 1996.

66: ibid.

67: John Nichols, "The English Lesson," *The Progressive*, June, 1997.

68: Interview with John Pagini, Alliance media director, Sept. 23, 1997.

69: ibid.

70: Jim Anderton, "Sack the Radio NZ Board for Incompetence," party statement, June 16, 1999.

71: Sandra Lee, statement, Oct. 8, 1999.

72: Jim Anderton, statement, Sept. 26, 1999.

73: ibid.

74: "How the Democrats Have Made the Difference," party document, 1998.

75: "New ABC Board Appointments," statement by Sen. Vicki Bourne, Sept. 8, 1999.

76: Debate Transcript, Australian Parliamentary Library, March 31, 1999.

77: ibid.

78: "Appointments to ABC Board: Democrats Call for Parliamentary Scrutiny," party statement, Feb. 5, 1998.

79: Bharati Ray, interview, Dec. 16, 1998.

CHAPTER THREE

1: See John Nichols, "Nader Tramps N.H. Roads Crusading For a New Politics," *The Toledo Blade*, Feb. 10, 1992.

2: ibid.

3: *The Concord Principles: An Agenda for a New Initiatory Democracy*, Ralph Nader, Feb. 1, 1992.

4: Interview with Vicky Turner, Feb. 6, 1992.

5: Interview with Arnie Arnsesen, Feb. 6, 1992.

6: Gaylord Nelson, interview, Oct. 8, 1999.

7: ibid.

8: Letter to Reed Hundt, chairman, Federal Communications Commission, Feb. 8, 1995.

9: Ira Teinowitz, "Branding PSAs Could Prove to Be Costly: Wooden," *Advertising Age*, June 29, 1999, p. 16.

10: Bill McConnell, "FCC in Direct Line of Fire from Hill," *Broadcasting & Cable*, March 15, 1999, p. 19.

11: See: www.fair.org/activism/organize/html

12: "Local 142 Fights Newspaper Closure," *The Dispatcher*, monthly newspaper of the ILWU, October, 1999, P. 7.

13: "S.F. Pol May Seek Suit to Stop Sale of Paper," *Editor & Publisher*, December 4, 1999, P. 14.

14: Karen Kubby, interviews, July, 1999.

15: David Hatch, "Kids Docs Call TV and Tots a Dangerous Duo," *Electronic Media*, August 9, 1999, p. 1A.

16: L. Brent Bozell III, "Networks Cover Pro Wrestling Over Chinese Espionage," *The Wall Street Journal*, July 6, 1999, p. A14; P. J. Bednarski, "On Smut Patrol With the PTC's Brent Bozell," *Electronic Media*, May 31, 1999, p. 14.

17: David Cay Johnson, "Gap Between Rich and Poor Found Substantially Wider," *The New York Times*, September 5, 1999, p. 14.

18: David E. Rosenbaum, "Congress Leaves Business Groups Almost All Smiles," *The New York Times*, November 26, 1999, pp. A1, A26.

19: Bernie Sanders, *Outsider in the House* (London: Verso, 1997), pp. 231-32.

20: "21st Century Media: Media Manifesto of the Campaign for Press and Broadcast Freedom," June, 1996.

21: Barbara Ehrenreich, interview, Oct. 20, 1999.

22: Paul Wellstone, interview, January 9, 1999.

23: John Conyers, interview, March, 1998.

24: Patty Allen, interview, Oct. 11, 1999.

25: Janine Jackson, "Moribund Militants: Corporate Media on (Re)organized Labor," *Extra!*, January/February, 1996.

ABOUT THE AUTHORS

Robert W. McChesney is a professor of communication at the University of Illinois at Urbana-Champaign. He is the author of six other books on the media, including *Rich Media, Poor Democracy: Communication Politics in Dubious Times* (New Press, 2000).

John Nichols is editorial page editor of *The Capital Times* in Madison, WI. A Nation Institute fellow, he writes "The Beat," a regular column for *The Nation* magazine. He has covered four U.S. presidential elections, and has written about politics and policy from South Africa, Zimbabwe, India, Israel, El Salvador and more than a dozen other countries.

Barbara Ehrenreich is the author of many books, including *Blood Rites: Origins and History of the Passions of War* and *Fear of Falling: The Inner Life of the Middle Class.*

Ralph Nader is a consumer activist and the 2000 Green Party presidential candidate.

Paul Wellstone has represented the state of Minnesota as a U.S. Senator since 1990.